A Bibliography and
Reader's Guide to the
First Editions of
P.G. Wodehouse
2nd Edition

A Bibliography and Reader's Guide to the First Editions of
P.G. Wodehouse
2nd Edition

DAVID A. JASEN

Greenhill Books

Greenhill
Books

Second, Revised and Expanded edition of
*A Bibliography and Reader's Guide to
the First Editions of P. G. Wodehouse*
first published 1986 by Greenhill Books,
Lionel Leventhal Limited, 2–6 Hampstead High Street,
London NW3 1QQ.

ISBN 0-947898-18-2

Publishing History
*A Bibliography and Reader's Guide to
the First Editions of P. G. Wodehouse*
was first published in 1970 by Archon Books,
Hamden, Connecticut, and in 1971 by Barrie & Jenkins,
London, England

Greenhill Books
welcome readers' suggestions for books that might
be added to this Series. Please write to us if
there are titles which you would like to recommend.

Printed by Antony Rowe Limited
Chippenham, Wiltshire.

To my Wife

Susan,

with Love and Affection

PREFACE
TO THE SECOND EDITION

The purpose of the original *Bibliography and Reader's Guide to the First Editions of P. G. Wodehouse* was first, to note those characteristics which would identify the first editions of his books and second, to present the characters and places and things which would help to recall the plot or stories in detail. Only in this way could the various relationships be catalogued from one book or story to another.

Much has happened since the original *Bibliography* was published in 1970. Plum had six more books to write, his stories were filmed for television by the BBC, and he was knighted by Queen Elizabeth II just six weeks before his death at the age of 93 on February 14, 1975. His centennial was celebrated in both his adopted home in the United States and in England with exhibitions of his work.

I should like to thank John Fletcher and Robert A. Hall, Jr. for their help in this new edition.

David A. Jasen, 1986

PREFACE
TO THE FIRST EDITION

Pelham Grenville Wodehouse, the most prolific humorist of the twentieth century, was born on October 15, 1881, in Guildford, England and became a United States citizen on December 16, 1955. His first published book appeared in 1902, his most recent in 1969. In addition to the ninety-one volumes covered in this work, he has written a number of plays and musical comedies. His writings have been widely translated. One measure of the regard in which he has been held was the award to him in 1939 of the degree of Doctor of Letters by Oxford University.

This present volume attempts in the first instance to provide identification of Wodehouse's first editions suitable for collectors and bibliographers. No one has a complete collection of the editions described here — until 1915 first printings did not exceed 2,000 copies.

In the second place this work lists and briefly characterizes persons and places in Wodehouse's novels and stories. The indexes will readily assist the reader to follow characters through the many stories in which they appear. As best any simple listing can, they will introduce the reader to a world of much imagination and fun.

1970

Publisher's Note: The books are listed chronologically, by date of publication. Numbers in parentheses before characters or places listed indicate the page of the book on which the character or place is first mentioned.

TABLE OF CONTENTS

CHRONOLOGICAL LIST OF TITLES*

*Titles in capital letters are books, those in small type are short stories.

1

2

3

4

7

1 – THE POTHUNTERS

First published September 18 1902 by Adam & Charles Black, London, 272 pages. Bound in royal blue cloth, lettered and decorated in silver with a frontispiece and nine illustrations by R. Noel Pocock. No advertisements. A later edition was issued with sheets of the first, but it contains eight pages of advertisements, headed "Beautiful Books for Young People."

Characters

(13)   Tony Graham – Merevale's House at St. Austin's
(13)   Allen Thomson – Tony's cousin at Rugby
(15)   Jim Thomson – Allen's brother in Merevale's House
(19)   Dawkins – St. Austin's Gym Instructor
(31)   J. George Welch – Half-mile winner in Merevale's
(31)   Reginald Robinson – Tony Graham's fag in Merevale's
(43)   Morrison – Friend of Robinson's and fag in Ward's House
(44)   Dimsdale – Fag in School House
(45)   Scott – Fag in School House
(48)   Reade – Shares study with Barrett in Philpott's House
(48)   Barrett – Shares study with Reade and collects birds eggs
(48)   Dallas – Member of Ward's House
(48)   Vaughan – Member of Ward's House
(49)   Mr. Ward – Master at St. Austin's
(51)   Simpson – Fag
(56)   Mr. Thompson – Master of the 6th Form
(57)   Biffen – Ground Man at St. Austin's
(67)   (Babe) Robert MacArthur – Day boy
(67)   (The Mutual Friend) Plunkett – Head of Ward's House and shares study with Vaughan and Dallas
(87)   Galloway – Member of Ward's House
(95)   (Alderman) Charteris – Shares study with Welch in Merevale's and edits the unofficial monthly magazine, *The Glow Worm*
(99)   Jackson – Contributor to *The Glow Worm* who lives in Dawson's
(105) Adamson – Member of Dawson's
(111) R. St. H. Grey – Member in Prater's House
(125) Saunders and Ned – Badgwick Hall gameskeepers
(134) Detective Inspector Roberts – from Scotland Yard
(151) Perkins – Master of the Upper Fourth form

(151) Merevale — Master at St. Austin's
(168) (The Moke) William — Merevale's butler
(184) Parker — The Headmaster's butler
(184) The Rev. Herbert Perceval — Headmaster of St. Austin's
(196) Sir Alfred Venner, M.P. — Owner of Badgwick Hall, near the school grounds
(221) Stokes — Burglar who stole school cups

Places

(14)   Aldershot — Where boxing competition was held
(15)   St. Austin's — School where main action of story is told
(31)   School House — Boarding house at St. Austin's
(31)   Merevale House — Boarding house at St. Austin's
(43)   Ward House — Boarding house at St. Austin's
(48)   Philpott House — Boarding house at St. Austin's
(99)   Dawson's House — Boarding house at St. Austin's
(114) Dacre's House — Boarding house at St. Austin's
(168) Prater's House — Boarding house at St. Austin's
(169) Halliday's House — Boarding house at St. Austin's
(214) Perkins' House — Boarding house at St. Austin's

2 – A PREFECT'S UNCLE

First published September 11 1903 by Adam & Charles Black, London, 264 pages. Bound in red cloth, lettered and decorated in gold, black, lavender, and pink with a frontispiece and seven illustrations by R. Noel Pocock.

Characters

(1)	Marriott – Prefect of Leicester's House at Beckford College who shares a study with Gethryn
(1)	William – Butler and bootboy at Leicester's House
(5)	(The Bishop) Alan Gethryn – Head of Leicester's and superb cricketer
(5)	The Rev. James Beckett – Headmaster of Beckford College
(9)	Miss Jones – Matron at Leicester's
(10)	Jack Monk – Member of Leicester's
(10)	Danvers – Member of Leicester's and a friend of Monk's
(11)	Reece – Member of Leicester's and cricketer
(11)	Waterford – Member of Leicester's
(16)	Skinner – A fag at Leicester's
(18)	P.V. Wilson – Marriott's fag in Leicester's in the Lower Fourth.
(21)	Norris – Head of Jephson's and Captain of the cricket team.
(21)	Samuel Wilberforce Gosling – A day boy who plays cricket well
(21)	Miles – The school's professional Cricket Instructor
(22)	Pringle – Member of School House also on the cricket team
(25)	Baynes – Good cricket player
(27)	Mr. Jephson – School Master also in charge of cricket
(31)	Reginald Farnie – Gethryn's younger uncle also at Leicester's. Belongs to the Upper Fourth form.
(49)	Mr. Strudwick – Master of the Lower Fourth form
(52)	Watson – Groundman at Beckford College
(55)	Lorimer – Shares study with Pringle in the School House. Belongs to the Upper Fourth form.
(70)	Millett – A Junior in Leicester's
(71)	Smith – Member of Markham's from whom Farnie bought a bicycle
(78)	Baker – Shares a study with Norris in Jephson's
(144)	Mr. Robertson – Master at Beckford College
(153)	Col. Ashby – Friend of Pringle's father
(187)	Gregson – Member of Leicester's

(188) Lee — Member of Leicester's
(188) Adams — Member of Leicester's
(188) Bond — Member of Leicester's
(188) Brown — Member of Leicester's
(188) Burgess — Member of Leicester's
(189) Crowninshaw — Member of Leicester's
(189) Chamberlain — Member of Leicester's
(189) Carstairs — Member of Leicester's
(220) Mortimer Wells — Friend of the Headmaster's who is one judge in the poetry competition
(222) Mr. Lawrie — Master of the Sixth form
(229) Mr. Sims — Master of the Upper Fifth form

Places

(1)   Beckford College — Public school where main action of story is laid
(1)   Leicester's House — Boarding house at Beckford's
(7)   School House — Boarding house at Beckford's
(7)   Jephson's — Boarding house at Beckford's
(29)   Horton — Railroad station near Beckford
(71)   Markham's — Boarding house at Beckford's
(72)   Biddlehampton — Village near Beckford's
(72)   Cow and Cornflower — Pub at Biddlehampton
(104) Anfield — Village 15 miles from Beckford's
(132) *Comic Blitherings* — Comic weekly read by Farnie
(144) Robertson's — Boarding house at Beckford's
(154) Charchester — Rival school
(189) Webster's — Boarding house at Beckford's
(195) Browning's — Boarding house at Beckford's
(201) Pudford — Village
(201) Little Bindlebury — Village
(205) Little Bindlebury Arms — Pub in the village

3 – TALES OF ST. AUSTIN'S

First published November 10 1903 by Adam & Charles Black, London, 284 pages. Bound in light red pictorial cloth, lettered and decorated in gold, yellow, black, and lavender with a frontispiece and eleven illustrations by T.M.R. Whitwell, R. Noel Pocock, and E.F. Skinner.

Short Stories and essays of public school life.

How Pillingshot Scored

Characters

Pillingshot
Mr. Mellish — Master
Parker — Pillingshot's friend
Smythe — In the same house as Pillingshot
M. Gerard — French Master
Scott — In the First Eleven
Mr. Yorke — Master
Young Brown – Carried on a stretcher
Venables — Member of Merevale's House, Captain of the cricket team and a friend of Scott's

The Odd Trick

Characters

Philip St. H. Harrison — Member of Merevale's
Tony Graham — Prefect of Merevale's
Braithwaite — Member of Merevale's
Mace — Member of Merevale's
Scott — Cricketer
Charteris — Cricketer
Welch — Captain of Merevale's cricket team
Merevale — House Master

L'Affaire Uncle John

Characters

Richard Venables — Captain of St. Austin's cricket team
Archibald Venables — Richard's brother at King's College, Cambridge

13

Biffen — Groundsman
John Dalgliesh — Richard's uncle
Sir Everard Venables — Richard's father
Mrs. James Anthony — Richard's sister
Welch — Cricketer
Scott — Cricketer
Lord Marmaduke Twistleton — Guarantees Richard a job as
    land agent.

Harrison's Slight Error

Characters

P. St. H. Harrison — Member of Merevale's
Mace
Babington — Member of Dacre's House
Barrett — Member of Philpott's House
Grey
Venables — Head of Merevale's House and Captain of the cricket
    team
The Moke — Butler and bootboy at Merevale's
Young Venables

Bradshaw's Little Story

Characters

"I"
Frederick Wackerbath Bradshaw — Member of Prater's, a junior
Mr. Mellish — Form Master
Kendal — Junior
White
Yorke — Master of Upper Fifth
Prater — House Master

A Shocking Affair

Characters

"I" — Member of Prater's, a junior
F.W. Bradshaw
Mr. Mellish — Form Master
Brown — A junior
Morrison — A junior

14

M. Gerard — French Master
Blaize — Science and Chemistry Master

The Babe and The Dragon

Characters

(Babe) MacArthur
(The Dragon) Miss Florence Beezley — Friend of Babe's sister
    at Girton
Charteris — Prefect at Merevale's
Dacre — House Master

Magazines: *The Glow Worm; The Austinian*

The Manoeuvres of Charteris

Characters

Old Crockfordians — Cricket team composed of riff-raff from
    that Village
Charteris — Member of Merevale's
Graham — Charteris' friend who got injured playing football
(Babe) MacArthur — Member of Merevale's and Captain of
    football team
Merevale — House Master and head of football
Thomson — Member of football team
Welch — Shares study in Merevale's with Charteris and member
    of football team
Bannister — Member of football team
Prescott — Captain of Dacre's football team
Mr. Prater — House Master
P. St. H. Harrison
Headmaster
Dr. Adamson — College Doctor who lives in Stapleton
Secretary of the Old Crockfordians — A ruffian
"Charles his friend"
Crowninshaw — Charteris' fag
Parker — Headmaster's butler
Dorothy — Headmaster's niece

15

Places and Things

Stapleton — Town near St. Austin's
Worbury — Village near Badgwick Hall
Rutton — Village eight miles from Stapleton
Stapleton Herald — newspaper

How Payne Bucked Up

Characters

Charles Augustus Walkinshaw — Acting Captain and Secretary
   of football team
Grey — Captain of football team
Reade — Philpott's — Member of football team
Barrett — Philpott's — Member of football team
Payne — Dacre's — Member of football team
Bowden — Member of football team who shares study with
   Payne

Author!

Characters

Jack S.M. Babington — Member of Dacre's
Mr. Reginald Seymour — Substitute Math teacher
Peterson — Babington's friend
Jenkins — Babington's friend
Babington's older cousin at Guy's
Richards — Friend of Babington's cousin

The Tabby Terror

Characters

Captain Kettle — Prater's cat
Smith — Member of Prater's
Montgomery — Shares study with Smith
Shawyer — Friend of Smith and Montgomery
Dick Trentham — Head of house
Mrs. James Williamson — Trentham's sister

16

The Prize Poem

Characters

Reynolds — Remove
Smith — Sixth form
Montgomery — Sixth form
Morrison — Sixth form
Evans — Morrison's fag
The Rev. Arthur James Perceval — Headmaster
Mrs. Perceval — Headmaster's wife
Mr. Wells — Perceval's college chum and judge of poetry contest

Essays

"Work"
"Notes"
"Now, Talking About Cricket"
"The Tom Brown Question"

4 — THE GOLD BAT

First published September 13 1904 by Adam & Charles Black, London, 280 pages. Bound in dark red pictorial cloth, lettered and decorated in gold, black, light blue and yellow with a frontispiece and seven illustrations by T.M.R. Whitwell.

A novel of public school life, Wrykyn, the school where the story is laid, is based on Wodehouse's alma mater. The plot centers around the struggles for the last vacancy on the football fifteen and the doings of a mysterious "League" in the school.

Characters

(3)   Otway — Member of First Fifteen
(4)   Maurice — Member of First Fifteen
(4)   Robinson — Member of First Fifteen
(4)   Dick Trevor — Head of Donaldson's and Captain of First Fifteen
(4)   Clephane — Member of First Fifteen
(5)   Clowes — Member of Donaldson's, on the First Fifteen and close friend of Trevor's
(5)   Rand-Brown — Member of Seymour's
(6)   Paget — Ex-head of Donaldson's
(11) Barry — Member of Seymour's who shares Study 6 with M'Todd
(17) Donough O'Hara — Member of Dexter's who lost Trevor's Gold Bat
(18) Mr. Robert Dexter — House Master
(24) Ruthven — Member of Dexter's
(27) Moriarty — Member of Dexter's and friend of O'Hara's
(28) Headmaster of Wrykyn
(28) Sir Eustace Briggs — Mayor of Wrykyn
(30) M. Gandinois — French Master
(33) Smith — School porter
(38) M'Todd — Member of Seymour's who shares Study 6 with Barry
(39) Crawford — Member of School House
(43) Drummond — Member of Seymour's who shares Study 5 with De Bertini. Barry's friend.
(48) Mill — Member of Seymour's and Prefect
(54) Master Thomas Renford — Milton's fag
(56) Raoul de Bertini (Bertie) — Shares study at Seymour's with Drummond

18

(61)	Milton – Head of Seymour's also on Football Committee
(61)	Allardyce – On Football Committee
(67)	Mr. Seymour – House Master and Football Master at Wrykyn
(82)	Mr. Banks – Mathematics Master
(82)	Mr. Morgan – Mathematics Master
(85)	Harringay – Head of form in Mathematics
(91)	Gregson – Member of Day's
(95)	Harvey – Redford's friend and owner of ferrets
(107)	(Shoeblossom) James Rupert Leather-Twigg – Member of Seymour's in Study 7
(114)	Herbert – Boot and knife boy at Seymour's
(124)	Strachan – Member of Day's and First Fifteen
(138)	Rigby – Prefect in Seymour's
(159)	Linton – Member of Seymour's
(159)	Griffith – Member of Seymour's
(159)	Hunt – Member of Seymour's
(159)	Kershaw – Member of Seymour's
(159)	Chapple – Member of Seymour's
(162)	Mr. Aldridge – Master and referee of school football match
(165)	Dr. Oakes – School doctor
(178)	Jevons – Captain of Ripton School football team
(189)	Master Samuel Menzies – Member of Seymour's
(202)	Mr. Day – House Master also in charge of the gymnasium
(220)	Butler to Headmaster
(269)	Charles Mereweather Cook – Day boy

Places and Things

(2)	Wrykyn – Public school half mile from that town
(2)	*Wrykinian* – School magazine
(5)	Donaldson's – Boarding house at Wrykyn's
(5)	Seymour's – Boarding house at Wrykyn's
(9)	Ripton – Rival school
(17)	Dexter's – Boarding house at Wrykyn's
(22)	School House – Boarding house at Wrykyn's
(50)	*Sportsman* – Mass circulation magazine
(78)	*Wrykyn Patriot* – Town's newspaper
(91)	Day's – Boarding house at Wrykyn's
(120)	Templar's – Boarding house at Wrykyn's
(121)	Appleby's – Boarding house at Wrykyn's
(215)	Chesterton – Town two miles from Wrykyn
(274)	Bryant's – Boarding house at Wrykyn's
(275)	Aldershot – Place for sporting competitions

5 — WILLIAM TELL TOLD AGAIN

First published November 11 1904 by Adam & Charles Black, London, 108 pages. Bound in brown pictorial cloth, lettered and decorated in gold, black, green, and yellow with frontispiece and illustrations in full color by Philip Dadd. Reprints which at first glance resemble the first edition are undated and give the publisher's address on the title page.

This is the children's classic retold.

6 – THE HEAD OF KAY'S

First published October 5 1905 by Adam & Charles Black, London, 280 pages. Bound in dark red pictorial cloth, lettered and decorated in gold, black, yellow, and grey-blue with a frontispiece and seven illustrations by T.M.R. Whitwell.

Characters

(1)	Jimmy Silver – Head of Blackburn's and Captain of its cricket team and also on football team
(1)	Robert Mowbray Fenn – Head of Kay's and all-round cricketer
(3)	Kennedy – Prefect of Blackburn's on First Eleven and switched to Head of Kay's
(3)	Challis – Member of Blackburn's on First Eleven
(7)	Williams – Prefect of Blackburn's who plays a Cakewalk on the piano
(7)	Billy Silver – Jimmy's brother who lives in Kay's
(10)	Kay – Housemaster
(16)	Blackburn – Housemaster
(29)	Wayburn – Member of Kay's and cricketer
(29)	Walton – Member of Kay's, bad fellow and cricketer
(42)	Morrell – Member of Mulholland's
(43)	Mulholland – Housemaster and Music Master
(55)	The Bishop of Rumtifoo – Distributed prizes at end of term
(63)	Mortimer – Member of Kay's who attended camp
(63)	Perry – Member of Kay's and Walton's friend who attended camp
(63)	Callingham – Member of Kay's who attended camp
(65)	Wren – Member of Kay's who attended camp
(76)	Leveson – Member of Kay's who attended camp
(77)	Private Jones – Sentry at camp
(111)	Matron – of Kay's
(136)	Spencer – Kennedy's fag in Kay's
(142)	MacPherson – Member of Kay's football team
(162)	Fenn – Robert Fenn's older brother attending King's College in Cambridge. Playwright.
(163)	Higgs – An actor-manager who stars in Fenn's opera
(175)	Mr. Raynes – Housemaster
(186)	Thomas Edward – Matron's cat at Kay's
(223)	Taylor – Fenn's fag at Kay's

(224) Baker — Silver's fag at Blackburn's
(236) Watson — Headmaster's butler
(256) Dencroft — Housemaster who took over from Kay

Places

(1)   Kay's — Boarding house at Eckleton
(2)   Blackburn's — Boarding house at Eckleton
(2)   School House — Boarding house at Eckleton
(2)   Bedell's (Beddell's) — Boarding house at Eckleton
(2)   Mulholland's — Boarding house at Eckleton
(8)   Eckleton — Public school where action takes place
(48)   Composers — Gotsuchakoff and Thingummyowsky
(57)   Aldershot — Camp for cadets
(58)   Cove Reservoir — Bathing hole at Aldershot
(168) Eckleton's Theatre
(228) Tuppenham — Rival school
(263) Blair's — Boarding house at Eckleton
(269) Gay's — Boarding house at Eckleton
(274) Denny's — Boarding house at Eckleton
(276) Ledby — Village three and half miles from school

7 – LOVE AMONG THE CHICKENS

First published June 1906 by George Newnes Ltd., London, 312 pages. Bound in stone-colored cloth, lettered and decorated in stone, green, and orange with a frontispiece and three illustrations by H.M. Brock.

Wodehouse's first novel for adults contains humor in a love story. The only novel featuring Ukridge.

Characters

(1)	Jeremy Garnet - Hero — author of two published novels, ex-schoolmaster with Ukridge, and wants to marry Phyllis
(1)	Mrs. Medly — Garnet's landlady
(9)	Lickford — Writer and painter friend of Garnet's
(13)	Stanley Featherstonehaugh Ukridge — 6' 2" loveable scoundrel who wears old grey flannel suit with pince-nez and gingerbeer wire plus mackintosh. Favorite expression is "old horse."
(14)	Millie Ukridge — Stanley's wife
(32)	Phyllis Derrick - Heroine — loved by Jerry
(32)	Patrick Derrick — Phyllis' father who is professor at Dublin University
(34)	Albert — Youth in train with Aunty and 20 year old sister
(34)	Aunty — Travelling with Albert
(38)	Molly McEachern — Phyllis' friend who gave her Jerry's book
(45)	Bob — Beale's mongrel dog
(51)	Beale — Red-headed ex-sergeant who is handyman on the chicken farm
(51)	Mrs. Beale — Beale's wife and the farm's cook
(84)	Tom Chase — Lieutenant in the Royal Navy who is engaged to Norah. A fancy talker like Psmith.
(93)	Dawlish — Grocer at Lyme Regis
(99)	Edwin — Millie's pure-bred Persian cat
(118)	Norah Derrick — Phyllis' sister engaged to Tom Chase
(130)	Farmer Leigh — Neighbor near Up Lyme to Chicken farm
(133)	Harry Hawk — Boatman hired by Jerry to throw Prof. Derrick overboard
(154)	Vickers — Butcher in Lyme Regis
(184)	Curtis — Fishmonger in Lyme Regis
(196)	Aunt Elizabeth — Millie's aunt who is Lady Lakenheath
(196)	Smith — Gramophone dealer in Dorchester

(201)   Jane Muspratt — Harry Hawk's fiancee
(304)   Mrs. Kathleen O'Brien — Phyllis' aunt who gave wedding
           reception
(304)   Mrs. Minchley — Mrs. O'Brien's cook
(304)   Mr. Hill — Mrs. O'Brien's butler

Places and Things

(1)   *The Manoeuvres of Arthur* — Garnet's novel
(22)   Lyme Regis — Chicken farm in Dorsetshire, main place of action
(58)   Cob — Beach spot in Lyme Regis
(135)   "Not Really a Coward" — Garnet's short story
(135)   "Hilda's Hero" — Garnet's short story
(138)   Net and Mackerel — Pub in Lyme Regis
(157)   *The Brown Haired Girl* — Projected title of Garnet's new novel
(163)   *The Outsider* — Garnet's novel
(163)   Bastable & Kirby — Publishers of *The Outsider*

7a – LOVE AMONG THE CHICKENS

First published May 11 1909 by Circle Publishing Company, New York, 350 pages. Bound in light brown cloth, lettered and decorated in blue-black and red with a frontispiece and five illustrations by Armand Both. This edition has numerous small changes in the text.

7b – LOVE AMONG THE CHICKENS

First published May, 1921 by Herbert Jenkins, London, 256 pages. Bound in blue cloth, lettered and decorated in dark blue, identifiable by the list of six Wodehouse titles on the verso of the half-title page which must end with *Indiscretions of Archie*. "Entirely rewritten for this edition" appears on the title page.

8 – THE WHITE FEATHER

First published October 9 1907 by Adam & Charles Black, London, 284 pages. Bound in light brown cloth, lettered and decorated in black, gold, and white with frontispiece and eleven illustrations by William Townend. No advertisements at the end of the book.

A sequel to *The Gold Bat,* and the best novel of school life, with characters fully drawn.

Characters

(1)	Clowes – Visiting the Old School, now at Oxford
(1)	Allardyce – Captain of football
(1)	Trevor – Visiting the Old School, now at Oxford
(2)	Barry – Member of Seymour's
(3)	Attell – Member of Appleby's and cohort of Stanning
(5)	Stanning – Member of Appleby's, a bad fellow on the First Fifteen
(5)	Drummond – Member of Seymour's, featherweight at Aldershot and on the Second Eleven
(9)	Mr. Seymour – Housemaster and Gamemaster
(11)	Linton – Member of Seymour's
(16)	R.D. Sheen – Hero of story in Seymour's who has Study 12
(21)	Herbert – Seymour's bootboy
(23)	Mitchell – Former Wrykynian who lives at home in the town of Wrykyn
(27)	Dunstable – Member of Day's and Linton's friend
(28)	Menzies – Member of Seymour's who has Study 3
(33)	Albert – Town ruffian
(37)	Renford – A junior member of Seymour's
(39)	Sir William Bruce – Conservative candidate for Mayor of Wrykyn; old Wrykinian
(39)	Jack Bruce – Sir William's son who is a day boy in Engineering and drives auto
(39)	Saul Pedder – Radical candidate for Mayor
(42)	Sergeant Cook – Proprietor of refreshment establishment in Wrykyn
(43)	Mrs. Cook – Sergeant Cook's wife
(44)	McTodd – Member of Seymour's and Barry's friend
(57)	Mason – Member of Appleby's
(60)	Harvey – Junior member of Seymour's

(60)   Watson – Junior member of Seymour's
(60)   Rigby – Head of Seymour's
(67)   Jackson – Junior at Dexter's
(68)   Painter – Junior at Dexter's and friend of Jackson
(69)   Bowick – Junior at Dexter's
(69)   Crowle – Junior at Dexter's
(69)   Tomlin – Junior at School House
(75)   Joe Bevan – Lightweight champ of the world. Teaches boxing
             to Sheen.
(101)   Francis "Frank" Hunt – Boxer in training with Bevan
(110)   George Jenkins – Boxing instructor at Wrykyn
(115)   Mr. Spence – Cricket and gymnasium Master
(115)   Harrington – Member of School House
(170)   Keith – Captain of football at Ripton
(196)   Mill – Member of Seymour's
(288)   Biddle – Entered at Aldershot competition for Wrykyn
(267)   Clayton – Member of Seymour's and President of Court-martial

Places and Things

Wrykyn – School where the action takes place
(1)   Ripton – Rival school
(2)   Greenburgh – Rival school
(8)   Aldershot – Where Public School competitions are held
(12)   St. Jude's – School in the High Street in Wrykyn
(17)   Gotford Scholarship – In-school at Wrykyn
(42)   Cook's – Refreshment shop in Wrykyn
(83)   The Blue Boar – Pub on bank of River Severn where Bevan
             trains fighters
(232)   Queen's Avenue Gymnasium – Where boxing competition took
             place at Aldershot

9 — NOT GEORGE WASHINGTON

First published October 18 1907 by Cassell and Company, London, 280 pages. Bound in red-brown cloth, lettered in gold with a colored frontispiece by John E. Sutcliffe.

This partly autobiographical novel is of Wodehouse's early journalistic life as shared with Herbert Westbrook, who collaborated. An unusual novel, having four narrators. Cloyster resembles Wodehouse and Eversleigh is partly Westbrook.

Characters

(1)	Margaret Goodwin — Engaged to Cloyster
(1)	James Orlebar Cloyster — Journalist
(2)	Ponto — Margaret's dog
(8)	Gunton-Cresswell — Margaret and Cloyster's friend
(40)	Mrs. Driver — Cloyster's first landlady
(53)	David Ossian Macrae — Cloyster's tutor at St. Gabriel's, Cambridge
(57)	Charles Fermin — Columnist on *The Orb*
(57)	Gresham — Writer on *The Orb*
(60)	Stanley Briggs — Musical comedy actor-manager
(62)	Julian Eversleigh — Advertising writer and Cloyster's friend
(64)	Vancott — Baker who is Eversleigh's landlord in Rupert St.
(83)	Malim— Sir George Grant's secretary in the Foreign Office
(84)	Kit Malim — Malim's wife
(92)	Tom Blake — Kit's brother who skippers a barge. Ghost of Cloyster's serious verse.
(97)	The Rev. John Hatten — Runs a boy's club in Lambeth. Ghost of Cloyster's fiction.
(108)	Sidney Price — Works for the Moon Assurance Company. Ghost of society stuff.
(137)	George Chandos — Pseudonym Cloyster wanted to use
(150)	Norah Perkins — Sid's girl friend
(157)	Ada Blake — Tom's wife
(157)	Nuppie and Albert — Blake's young helpers aboard the barges
(164)	Eve Eversleigh — Julian's cousin whom he marries
(255)	Fane — Columnist of the "People and Things" in *The Orb*
(266)	Richard Belsey — Briggs' valet

Places and Things

(1)	St. Martin's, Guernsey — Home of the Goodwin's

9a – NOT GEORGE WASHINGTON

First published April 10th, 1980 by Continuum Publishing Corp., New York, 214 pages. Bound in green boards, lettered in gold on spine. "1980" appears by itself on the verso of the title page.

Except for an Introduction by David A. Jasen in this edition, it is identical with number 9.

29

First published in June, 1908 by the Globe Publishing Company, London, 144 pages. A paperback issued in vermillion pictorial wrappers, lettered and decorated in white with illustrations by W.K. Haselden of the *Daily Mirror*. Subtitle: "A Literary Quick-Lunch for People Who Have Got Five Minutes to Spare."

A compilation taken from the column "By the Way" by Wodehouse and Herbert Westbrook which appeared in the pink evening newspaper, *The Globe*. It consists of extremely dated topical humor.

11 – THE SWOOP!

First published April 16 1909 by Alston Rivers, Ltd., London, 128 pages. A paperback issued in white pictorial wrappers with an orange-red background, lettered and decorated in black and white with illustrations by C. Harrison. Subtitle: "How Clarence Saved England."

The story of the invasion of England by the Germans and how England was saved by a boy scout.

Characters

(9)	Clarence MacAndrew Chugwater — 14 year old Chief Scout of the Boy Scouts and junior sub-reporter for a London evening paper
(11)	Mr. Chugwater — Clarence's father
(12)	Mrs. Chugwater — Clarence's mother
(12)	Reggie Chugwater — Clarence's elder brother
(12)	Ralph Peabody — Grace's fiance
(12)	Alice — Clarence's sister
(12)	Horace Chugwater — Another brother
(12)	Grace — Clarence's sister
(18)	Prince Otto — Invader from Saxe-Pfenning, Germany
(18)	Captain the Graf von Poppenheim — Invader with Prince Otto
(21)	Grand Duke Vodkakoff — Russian invader
(21)	Mad Mullah — Invader from Somaliland
(60)	Private William Buggins — Boyscout
(62)	Wagstaff — Scout master
(76)	Private Biggs — Boyscout

Places and Things

(15)	Nasturtium Villa — The Chugwater home in Essex
(55)	Aldwych Site — Boyscout camp in London
(79)	*The Encore* — Music-hall weekly newspaper
(118)	Bachelor's — A London Club

First published September 15 1909 by Adam & Charles Black, London, 340 pages. Bound in olive-green cloth, lettered and decorated in black, red, and white with a frontispiece and eleven illustrations by T.M.R. Whitwell. The last part published separately under the title *Enter Psmith* in 1935. In 1953 Herbert Jenkins revised slightly and published the first part as *Mike at Wrykyn* and the last part as *Mike and Psmith*.

Faintly autobiographical, as one character called Westbrook taught at King-Hall's, a private school in Emsworth, Hampshire. So did Herbert Westbrook, and Wodehouse used to stay at King-Hall's quite often. Here also Wodehouse got the name Emsworth from which he named the Ninth Earl in a later saga. The longest public school novel – in fact two novels combined, since from the entrance of Psmith to the end is a story which can stand by itself.

Characters

(1)	Mrs. Jackson – Mike's mother
(1)	Marjory Jackson – Mike's sister aged 14
(1)	Reggie Jackson – Mike's brother
(2)	Mr. Jackson – Mike's father, an Old Wrykynian
(2)	Phyllis Jackson – Mike's sister
(2)	Mr. Wain – Housemaster at Wrykyn
(2)	Bob Jackson – An older brother aged 18 at Donaldson's House
(2)	Mike Jackson – Hero and member of Wain's House
(3)	Joe Jackson – Mike's famous brother and professional cricketer
(4)	Ella Jackson – Mike's sister
(4)	Gladys Maud Evangeline Jackson – Mike's 3 year old sister
(4)	Saunders – Professional cricketer and teacher to the Jackson boys
(7)	Uncle John – Mike's uncle
(8)	(Gazeka) Firby-Smith – Head of Wain's
(12)	James Wyatt – Wain's stepson, a friend of Mike's in the First Eleven
(17)	Miss Payne – Matron of Wain's
(20)	Billy Burgess – Captain of the school Cricket team
(23)	Westbrook – Master at King-Hall's
(37)	Trevor – Member of Donaldson's
(37)	Clowes – Member of Donaldson's
(42)	Henfry – On First Eleven

(48)   Constable Alfred Butt — Policeman in Wrykyn
(50)   Headmaster
(54)   Neville-Smith — Day boy at Wrykyn
(57)   Willoughby — Day boy at Wrykyn in the Lower Fifth
(57)   Brown — Day boy at Wrykyn
(57)   Mr. Spence — Master of Lower Fifth and Cricket Master
(58)   Mr. Seymour — Master of Lower Fourth and Housemaster
(59)   Mr. Shields — Master
(59)   Mr. Appleby — Master
(67)   Bates — School sergeant
(76)   Berridge — Cricketer on the First Eleven
(76)   Marsh — Cricketer on the First Eleven
(76)   Morris — Cricketer on the First Eleven
(80)   Reeves — Cricketer
(81)   Wilkins — Member of School House
(83)   Raikes — Member of Appleby's and cricketer
(89)   Burton — Member of Donaldson's
(97)   Ellerby — On First Eleven
(97)   Jenkins — Cricketer
(97)   Clephane — Day boy and cricketer
(100) (Shoeblossom) Leather-Twigg — Member of Seymour's who got
           chickenpox
(101) Dr. Oakes — School doctor
(129) Beverly — Day boy at Wrykyn
(150) Mr. Blenkinsop — Manager of the London & Oriental Bank
           where Wyatt works
(166) MacPherson — Manager of Mr. Jackson's sheep farm in Argentina
(174) Vicar Barlitt of Crofton
(176) Strachan — Captain of Wrykyn cricket team by default
(176) Sheen — Lightweight boxing champ for Wrykyn
(177) Mr. Outwood — Housemaster at Mike's at Sedleigh
(178) Rupert Psmith — Mike's good friend who lives at Lower Benford,
           Shropshire and came from Eton
(184) Spiller — Member of Outwood's and a Senior at Sedleigh
(187) Mr. Downing — Housemaster and Master of School Fire Brigade
           and Cricket
(191) Tom G. Jellicoe — Member of Outwood's, a Senior and roomate
           of Psmith and Jackson
(193) Robinson — Member of Outwood's, a Senior, cricketer and
           member of the Fire Brigade

33

(193) Stone — Member of Outwood's, a Senior, cricketer and member of the Fire Brigade
(197) Barnes — Head of Outwood's
(202) Adair — Member of Downing's, a natural leader who is Captain of cricket and football
(211) Prendergast — Member of village cricket team and played against Mike with the Free Forester's
(215) Sammy or Sampson — Mr. Downing's bull-terrior who gets painted red
(215) Wilson — Member of School House and Fire Brigade
(242) Dunster — Old Sedleighan who was at private school with Psmith and painted Sammy red.
(247) Mr. Barley — Landlord of the White Boar in Lower Borlock and member of the village cricket team
(254) Sergeant Collard — School sergeant
(256) MacPhee — Member of Downing's
(273) Markby — Groundsman for Sedleigh
(279) Edmund — Bootboy for Outwood's
(330) Barlow — Headmaster's butler

Places and Things

(2)   Wrykyn — Public School and main place of action for first half of book
(8)   East Wobsley — On the way to Wrykyn
(13)   Cook's — Teashop in Wrykyn
(16)   King Hall's — Mike's former private school in Emsworth, Hampshire
(64)   Worfield — Market town five miles from Wrykyn where they held a picnic
(65)   *Worfield Intelligencer & Farmer's Guide* — Newspaper
(65)   Grasshopper and Ant — Inn at Worfield
(85)   Geddington — Rival school in cricket
(104) *Wrykynian* — School magazine
(114) Ripton — Rival cricket and football school
(114) Wilborough — Rival cricket and football school
(114) Wain's — Boarding house at Wrykyn
(114) Donaldson's — Boarding house at Wrykyn
(114) School House — Boarding house at Wrykyn
(114) Appleby's — Boarding house at Wrykyn
(114) Seymour's — Boarding house at Wrykyn

34

(173) Sedleigh — Public School and main place of action for second
          half of book
(175) Outwood's — Mike's boarding house at Sedleigh
(177) The Jackson Home — Crofton, Shropshire — near Brindleford
(185) Psmith's Philosophy: "In this life, we must be prepared for
          every emergency. We must distinguish between the unusual
          and the impossible."
(188) Embury Hill — Two miles from Sedleigh where there is a
          Roman camp
(212) Lower Borlock — Village near school where Mike plays for the
          local cricket team
(247) White Boar — Inn at Lower Borlock
(305) Psmithism: "I should say that young Lord Antony Trefusis was
          in the soup already. I see the consomme splashing about his
          ankles."
(305) School House — Boarding house at Sedleigh
(305) Downings — Boarding house at Sedleigh

13 – THE INTRUSION OF JIMMY

First published May 11 1910 by W.J. Watt and Co., New York, 314 pages. Bound in black, lettered in gold with circular portrait in color pasted on. Frontispiece and four illustrations by Will Grefe.

Characters

(1)   Arthur Mifflin — Young leading actor who went to college with Pitt. Member of the Strollers'.
(2)   Willett — Musical comedy actor, member of the Strollers'
(2)   Raikes — Character actor and member of the Strollers'
(2)   James Willoughby Pitt — Hero who went to Yale, is expert in jewels, ex-reporter for the *News*, amateur boxer and road company actor. Loves Molly.
(3)   Sutton — Owner of the Majestic Theater and member of the Strollers'
(23)   John McEachern — A corrupt Captain of the New York City police force who is a widower with a daughter Molly
(26)   Molly McEachern — Heroine daughter of John, engaged to Lord Dreever but loves Jimmy
(30)   Rastus and Tommy — Molly's bulldogs
(39)   Spike Mullins — Burglar from the bowery, friend, follower and valet of Jimmy's
(65)   (Spennie) Hildebrand Spencer Poynt de Burgh John Hannasyde Coombe-Crombie — 12th Earl of Dreever, 24 year old Drone under the thumb of his aunt and uncle
(66)   Sir Thomas Blunt — Spennie's uncle and chairman of Blunt's Stores Ltd. Millionaire afraid of his wife.
(66)   Lady Julia Blunt — Sir Thomas' wife and Spennie's aunt with a forceful manner
(69)   Saunders — Butler at Dreever Castle
(92)   Hargate — Professional crooked billiard player and cardsharp
(94)   Charteris — Playwright, organizer and director of amateur theatricals at Dreever Castle
(180)   Samuel Galer — Detective sent by McEachern, posing as his friend from New York
(181)   ? — Detective sent by Sir Thomas, posing as his valet
(186)   Katie — Spennie's girlfriend whom he wishes to marry.

36

Places and Things

(1)   Strollers' Club — New York City theatrical club
(5)   *Love, The Cracksman* — Play starring Arthur Mifflin
(64)   Dreever Castle — Owned by the 12th Earl in Shropshire
(64)   Wragge's Detective Agency — London
(64)   Dodson's Private Inquiry Agency — London

13a – A GENTLEMAN OF LEISURE

First published November 15 1910 by Alston Rivers, Ltd., London, 352 pages. Bound in prussian blue cloth, lettered in gold. Minor changes in the text.

14 – PSMITH IN THE CITY

First published September 23 1910 by Adam & Charles Black, London, 268 pages. Bound in blue cloth, lettered and decorated in buff, white, and black with frontispiece and eleven illustrations by T.M.R. Whitwell.

This truly belongs to the public school books, but Psmith helps to bridge the gap. The bank portion is autobiographical and Mike's reactions were those of young Wodehouse.

Characters

(1)   Mr. John Bickersdyke – Old school friend of Mr. Smith's and manager of the New Asiatic Bank

(1)   Mike Jackson – Hero, cricket player extraordinary, Psmith's secretary and chum at the bank

(2)   Rupert Psmith – Mike's co-worker in the Postage Department at the bank

(2)   Mr. Smith – Psmith's very wealthy father

(6)   Bagley – Mr. Smith's groundman

(18)   John – Mike's bulldog

(30)   Mr. Waller – Head cashier of the bank, kind family man, widower and Socialist

(33)   Bannister – Fellow-worker in the bank

(33)   Mr. Rossiter – Head of Postage Department and Mike's first boss

(118)   Bristow – Replaced Mike in the Postage Dept. when Mike went To Cash

(149)   Edward Waller – 10 year old precocious son of the Cashier

(211)   Mr. Gregory – Head of the Fixed Deposits department

Places and Things

(2)   Ilsworth Hall – Owned by Mr. Smith

(22)   Dulwich – Village where Mike first boards

(22)   Dulwich College – In village where Mike gets an occasional game and Wodehouse's personal alma mater

(22)   Senior Conservative – Club whose members inclue Psmith, his father and Bickersdyke

(59)   Clement's Inn – Where Psmith and Mike share a flat

15 – THE PRINCE AND BETTY

First published February 14 1912 by W.J. Watt & Company, New York, 302 pages. Bound in black cloth, lettered in gold with two oval color portraits pasted on the front cover and with a frontispiece and four illustrations by Will Grefe.

A romantic novel written for the American market with Rupert Smith (without the "P") attending Harvard. The story deals with New York City slums, gang wars (one of the first to do so), and boxers. There is a brief episode in Mervo.

Characters

(1)	Elsa Keith – College chum of Betty's
(1)	Marvin Rossiter – Engaged to Elsa
(1)	Betty Silver – Heroine who loves John Maude. Typist for *Peaceful Moments*.
(2)	Benjamin Scobell – Betty's millionaire step-father who built a casino in Mervo. Also owned *Peaceful Moments* and a tenement on Broster Street.
(6)	John Maude – Hero who loves Betty. Went to Harvard with Smith and becomes Prince of Mervo.
(9)	Marion Scobell – Benjamin's spinster sister
(11)	Mrs. Jane Oakley – Scobell's wealthy and miserly aunt
(12)	General Poineau – Head of the Royalist Party in Mervo
(12)	M. d'Orby – President of the Republic of Mervo
(13)	Crump – Private secretary to Scobell
(23)	Andrew Westley – John's uncle
(26)	Jimmy Pitt – John's friend
(26)	Rupert Smith – College chum of John's who had worked for the *News* and then became Associate Editor of *Peaceful Moments*
(109)	J. Brabazon Renshaw – Editor-in Chief of *Peaceful Moments*
(112)	Luella Granville Waterman – Contributor to *Peaceful Moments*
(112)	Rev. Edwin T. Philpotts – Contributor to *Peaceful Moments*
(112)	B. Henderson Asher – Contributor to *Peaceful Moments*
(119)	Mrs. Julia Burdett Parslow – Contributor to *Peaceful Moments*
(120)	Pugsy Maloney – *Peaceful Moments* office boy
(126)	Bat Jarvis – Leader of the Groome St. gang and owns the Animal Fanciers Shop
(135)	Kid Brady – Light-weight boxer championed by *Peaceful Moments*

15a – PSMITH JOURNALIST

First published September 29 1915 by Adam & Charles Black, London, 248 pages. Bound in blue cloth, lettered and decorated in gold, black, yellow, and cream with a frontispiece and eleven illustrations by T.M.R. Whitwell.

In this version the love interest has been dropped and it becomes strictly a novel of adventure with Psmith and Mike Jackson in New York from Cambridge as members of their touring cricket team. Psmith becomes involved with slum conditions and gang wars. Minor changes in the text, with *Peaceful Moments* becoming *Cozy Moments*. The best version of the three. (See number 16)

40

16 – THE PRINCE AND BETTY

First published May 1 1912 by Mills & Boon, Ltd., London, 282 pages. Bound in red cloth, lettered in gold and black. The only Wodehouse title to be published by Mills & Boon.

Aside from the romance in the Mervian plot, this is a completely different story from number 15. The main scene is laid in a country house in Hampshire with a romantic setting. In this story, John Maude is English.

Characters

Elsa Keith — Betty's friend
Martin Rossiter — Engaged to Elsa
Betty Silver — Heroine
Benjamin Scobell — Betty's rich step-father
Lord Arthur Hayling — Betty's unsuccessful suitor and social
    arbitor to the Morrisons
John Maude — Hero who went to Cambridge
Marion Scobell — Benjamin's sister
General Poineau — Leader of Mervo's Royalist Party.
M. d'Orby — President of the Republic of Mervo
Edwin Crump — Scobell's secretary
Della Morrison — American secretary to Westley, Martin & Co.
    in London. Becomes an heiress
Andrew Westley — John's uncle who hates him
Jimmy Pitt — John's friend, mentioned in passing
Reeve-Smith — John's friend who went to Cambridge with him
Smith — John's friend who works for the *News*
Tom Spiller — Della's secret flame in New York
Mr. Richard Morrison — Della's father who loves baseball and is
    homesick for New York
Mrs. Morrison — Della's mother who tries to get into London's
    social whirl for Della's sake
Faraday — John's friend
Mr. Briggs — Butler at Norworth Court

Places and Things

Mervo — An island in the Mediterranean
Norworth Court — A castle in Hampshire rented by Lord
    Arthur for the Morrisons

17 – THE LITTLE NUGGET

First published August 28 1913 by Methuen & Co., London, 304 pages. Bound in red cloth, lettered and decorated in gold on spine. First edition stated on verso of title.

The scene takes place in a preparatory school with much of the action described from the point of view of an instructor. Ogden is the first of Wodehouse's spoiled brats.

Characters

(3)   (Nesta) Mrs. Elmer Ford – A wealthy divorced American who tries to kidnap her son Ogden

(4)   Lord Mountry – 28 year old amiable drone who went to Oxford with Peter

(10)   (The Little Nugget) Ogden Ford – 14 year old precocious and unpleasant son of Nesta's

(11)   Miss Cynthia Drassilis – Mercenary, callous fiancee of Peter's

(16)   Reggie Broster – Ogden's tutor at Mr. Ford's home

(19)   Mennick – Mr. Ford's private secretary

(23)   Audrey Blake - Mrs. Sheridan – Heroine who is a small, gracefully pretty girl of 25

(37)   Peter Burns – Hero engaged to Cynthia but only love was Audrey. Kind, good-looking and rich, becomes acting assistant master at Sanstead House. Tries to kidnap Ogden.

(42)   Mrs. Drassilis – Cynthia's hard, avaricious mother

(46)   Parker – Mrs. Drassilis' butler

(49)   Smith – Peter's valet

(63)   Arnold Abney – Owner and Headmaster of Sanstead House

(69)   Glossop – Gloomy assistant master at Sanstead House

(69)   White – Smooth Sam posing as butler at Sanstead House. Tries to kidnap Ogden.

(69)   Smooth Sam Fisher – Charming crook who tries to kidnap Ogden

(74)   Augustus Beckford – Lord Mountry's younger brother attending Sanstead House

(82)   Mrs. Attwell – Matron at Sanstead House

(86)   Buck MacGinnis – Crook from the Bowery who tries to kidnap Ogden

(87)   Miss Benjafield – Barmaid at The Feathers

(139)   Lefty – Crook with Buck's gang

42

Places and Things

(3)   Hotel Guelph — A London hotel where Mrs. Ford stayed
(61)   Sanstead House — Main scene of action. Preparatory school in
          Hampshire.
(86)   The Feathers — Local inn at Sanstead

17a — THE LITTLE NUGGET

First published January 10 1914 by W.J. Watt & Co., New York,
300 pages. Bound in black cloth, lettered and decorated in gold with a
frontispiece and two illustrations by Will Grefe. This edition must have
"Published January" beneath the copyright notice.

18 – THE MAN UPSTAIRS

First published January 23 1914 by Methuen & Co., London, 316 pages. Bound in brown cloth, lettered and decorated in gold on spine. First edition stated on verso of title.
Wodehouse's first book of short stories for adults.

The Man Upstairs

Characters

Annette Brougham – Heroine who is an impecunious young and pretty piano and voice teacher who composes
Alan Beverly – 28 year old hero who is wealthy and poses as an amateur painter
Reginald Sellers – Unsuccessful and snobbish painter
Epstein – Art agent
William Bates – Glasgow millionaire who poses as Alan Beverly
Grusczinsky and Buchterkirch – Annette's music publishers
Rupert Morrison – Author friend of Beverly's

Something To Worry About

Characters

Sally Preston – Londonite visiting Aunt Jane at Millbourne Bay, Hampshire
Thomas Kitchener – 25 year old second gardener who loves Sally
Jane Williams – Sally's aunt
Mr. Williams – Jane's husband
Ted Pringle – Sally's suitor
Albert Parsons – Sally's suitor
Arthur Brown – Sally's suitor
Joe Blossom – Sally's suitor
Constable Cobb – Village policeman

Deep Waters

Characters

George Barnert Callender – Hero who is an excellent swimmer at Marvis Bay and playwright of *Fate's Footballs*

Arthur Mifflin — Leading juvenile in *Fate's Footballs* who went to Cambridge with Callender

Mary Vaughan — Heroine who is an excellent swimmer and rescues Callender

When Doctors Disagree

Characters

Arthur Welch — Hero who is the barber at Hotel Belvoir
Maud Peters — Heroine who is the manicurist engaged to Arthur
Mr. "Skipper" Shute — American pugilist who likes Maud
Robert Bryce — Police-constable at White City

By Advice Of Council

Characters

(Jack Roach) Waiter — narrator
Traveller — deaf
Jerry Moore — Roach's friend who is a bit deaf
Gentleman Bailey — Roach's friend
Jane Tuxton — Engaged to Jerry

Rough-Hew Them How We Will

Characters

Paul Boielle — Waiter at Bredin's Parisian Cafe & Restaurant in Soho who paints
Jeanne Le Brocq — Avaricious waitress at Bredin's loved by Paul
M. Bredin — Owner of cafe
Young Man — General Manager of Galloway's Tried and Proven Braces who hires Paul as artist
Constable Thomas Parsons — London policeman

The Man Who Disliked Cats

Characters

"I" — Seated at the Cafe Brittannique in Soho
Jules Priaulx — Uncle and owner of the fashionable hotel in Paris of the same name
Jean Priaulx — Cashier at his uncle's hotel who wishes to paint; loves Marion

Alexander — A fat cat belonging to Mrs. Balderstone
   Rockmettler, an American staying at the Parisian hotel
Polly — Marion's parrott
Marion Henderson — Young English lady who owns Polly and
   wants Alexander
Captain Bassett — A Captain in the Guards who loves Marion
   and gives her Alexander
Paul Sartines — Man of letters who needs a secretary for his
   work: *History of the Cat in Ancient Egypt.*

Ruth In Exile

Characters

Ruth Warden — Heroine who is employed as a secretary-clerk
   in a pawn shop
M. Gandinot — Ugly-looking man who employs Ruth
Eugene Warden — Ruth's happy-go-lucky father
Bill — Warden's fox-terrier
George Vince — Hero — Wealthy and humorously talkative
   handsome young man who works for his father in the Vince
   Stores which specializes in childrens toys

Archibald's Benefit

Characters

Archibald Mealing — 31 year old amiable amateur golfer who is
   engaged to Margaret. Member of the Cape Pleasant Club in
   New Jersey.
McCay — Club secretary
Margaret Milsom — Engaged to Archie
Sigsbee — Member of Cape Pleasant and Sybarites' Club
Gossett — Unpleasant member of the Club who is a stock
   broker
Stuyvesant Milsom — Margaret's obnoxious brother
Mrs. Milsom — Margaret's mother

The Man, The Maid And The Miasma

Characters

Robert Ferguson — Employer

Roland Bean — A model, too-efficient office boy for Ferguson

Young Lady — Former girl friend of Ferguson's whom he still loves

The Good Angel

Characters

Keggs — The Keith's butler who runs a matrimonial sweepstake

Martin Rossiter — Hero who loves Elsa

Aubrey Barstowe — Author of "The Soul's Eclipse" and other poems who loves Elsa

Elsa Keith — Heroine

Tom Keith — Elsa's father

Mrs. Keith — Elsa's mother

Pots O' Money

Characters

Owen Bentley — Impecunious hero, an ex-cricketer who is a playwright and bank clerk

Mr. Shepperd — Audrey's father

Audrey Shepperd — Heroine who loves Owen

Mr. Dorman — Farmer in Shropshire where Owen went for a vacation

Prosser — Sociology professor who writes sentimental novels under the name of Edith Butler

Out Of School

Characters

James Datchett — 22 year old assistant master at Harrow House who wants to be an author

Frederick Knott — James' uncle

Blatherwick — Owner of a private school for small boys in Dover

Violet — Housemaid at Harrow House

Adolf — German youth working as odd-job man and black-mailing James.

Three From Dunsterville

Characters

Mary Hill — Heroine who is Joe's secretary
Eddy Moore — Villian who got Mary a job with Joe to spy for
him
Joe Rendal — Hero who loves Mary and is a financial broker
Harold — Joe's office boy

The Tuppenny Millionaire

Characters

George Albert Balmer — Employed by the Planet Insurance
Company
Harold Flower — Messenger for Planet
Lady Julia Waveney— Fires her paid companion
Young lady — Companion to Lady Julia who falls in love with
George

Ahead of Schedule

Characters

James Wilson — Rollo's valet who lived in Market Bumpstead
Rollo Finch — Amiable young drone who loves Miss Parker
Marguerite Parker — Chorus girl who marries Wilson
Andrew Galloway — Rollo's uncle, the Braces king who also
falls in love with Miss Parker

Sir Agravaine

Characters

Sir Agravaine the Dolorous — Knight at King Arthur's Court
who loves Yvonne
Yvonne — The Earl Dorm's daughter
Earl Dorm — Villainous father of Yvonne who keeps Sir
Agravaine prisoner

The Goal-Keeper And The Plutocrat

Characters

Isabel Rackstraw — Unofficially engaged to Clarence
The Hon. Clarence Tresillian — Loves Isabel and works as
  Footballer Jones
Lady Runnymede — Clarence's mother
Daniel Rackstraw — Isabel's millionaire father who is a football
  enthusiast

In Alcala

Characters

Rutherford Maxwell — Struggling English writer living in New
  York City who works for the New Asiatic Bank
Peggy Norton — Chorus girl who helps him with his play *Willie
  in the Wilderness*
Alice Halliday — Rutherford's girl friend in England
Winfield Knight — Actor who stars in "Willie"

19 – SOMETHING NEW

First published September 3 1915 by D. Appleton and Company, New York, 350 pages. Bound in red cloth, lettered and decorated in gold and turquoise with a frontispiece and three illustrations by F.R. Gruger. This edition may be identified by the numeral "1" on the bottom of the last page of the text.

The first of the Blandings Castle books, and often overlooked in discussions of the Blandings Saga, perhaps because it was published by Methuen in England, whereas Jenkins published the rest in the series. The novel concerns an alleged stolen scarab (pp. 55-80). Hilarious moments occur with the stealing of the scarab and "The Episode of the Great Collision" (pp. 233-257). The inner workings of the staff is discussed at length. Beach reminds one of Keggs.

Characters

(2)   Ashe Marson — 26 year old American hero who went to Harvard and Oxford. Writer of Gridley Quayle, Investigator series for the Mammoth Publishing Company's British Pluck Library under the name of Felix Clovelly. Physical culture addict and personal instructor to Mr. Peters. Loves Joan Valentine.

(9)   Mrs. Bell — Ashe's landlady in London

(12)   Joan Valentine — 23 year old pretty American heroine who writes short stories for Mammoth's *Home Gossip*. Had been a chorus girl in *The Baby Doll*, a governess and a lady's maid.

(23)   Hon. Frederick Threepwood — Bone-headed younger son of Lord Emsworth who was expelled from Eton and Oxford. Loves Joan but is engaged to Aline.

(23)   (Dickie) R. Jones — 50 year old fat moneylender and blackmailer

(24)   Clarence, The Earl of Emsworth — Freddie's wealthy, absent-minded father who paints his museum furniture and bedroom. Went to Eton in the 1860's and was nicknamed "Fathead." His museum includes such treasures as a Gutenberg Bible and a bullet from Waterloo. He is a member of the Senior Conservative Club in London. He loves flowers and is constantly pottering round his garden.

(27)   J. Preston Peters — American millionaire who collects scarabs

(27)   Aline Peters — Preston's daughter who is loved by Emerson but is engaged to Freddie

(28)	George Emerson — American redhead in a New York law firm who wants to marry Aline
(33)	Percy, Lord Stockheath – Freddie's cousin who had a breach-of-promise case and lost it
(40)	Adams — Head steward of the Senior Conservative Club
(48)	Rupert Baxter — Lord Emsworth's secretary who wears rimless glasses and suspects everyone
(59)	Thorne — Lord Emsworth's Scottish head gardener
(68)	Lord Bosham — Freddie's older brother
(98)	Simpson — Joan Valentine's pseudonym as Aline's maid
(128)	Lady Ann Warblington — Lord Emsworth's sister who has lived at Blandings since his wife died
(141)	Mrs. Twemlow — Housekeeper at Blandings
(141)	Beach — Lord Emsworth's Butler who has many ailments on which he discourses voluably in a most ungrammatical way
(162)	Merridew — Under-butler at Blandings
(162)	James — Footman at Blandings
(162)	Alfred — Footman at Blandings
(165)	Lady Mildred Mant — Lord Emsworth's eldest daughter and wife of Colonel Horact Mant
(165)	Colonel Horace Mant — Lady Mildred's husband of the Scots Guards
(165)	Judson — Freddie's valet
(216)	Algernon Wooster — Lord Stockheath's cousin
(216)	Bishop of Godalming — A Threepwood relative
(271)	Billy — Knife and shoe boy at Blandings
(286)	Muriel — Lady Ann's Persian cat
(288)	Dr. Bird — Local physician at Market Blandings
(338)	Slingsby — Chauffeur at Blandings

Places and Things

(2)	Number Seven, Arundel Street, Leicester Square, London — Ashe and Joan's rooming house
(4)	Mammoth Publishing Company — Ashe and Joan's employer
(13)	*Home Gossip* — Weekly paper published by Mammoth to which Joan contributes
(23)	Hotel Guelph, Piccadilly — Used by Freddie and Lord Emsworth
(23)	National Sporting Club — Freddie is a member

(26)   Blandings Castle — Ancestral home of Lord Emsworth, 70 miles from London. Noble pile of early Tudor buildings. Architecture was written up by Violett-le-Duc.

(39)   Senior Conservative Club — Lord Emsworth is one of 5,000 members

(76)   "The Adventures of the Secret Six" — A Gridley Quayle story

(100)   Mainprice, Mainprice & Boole — Law firm at 3 Denvers Street, Strand, founded in 1786

(118)   4:15 pm from Paddington — Express train to Blandings

(131)   Market Blandings — Sleepy village with a Norman church and a cinema over the grocer's shop

(182)   *Intelligencer and Echo* — Newspaper published in the neighboring town of Blatchford

(225)   Emsworth Arms — The best of the eleven inns or public houses in Market Blandings.

19a — SOMETHING FRESH

First published September 16 1915 by Methuen and Co., London, 320 pages. Bound in green cloth, lettered in black. First edition stated on verso of title.

This edition differs slightly from number 19. Ashe Marson and George Emerson are now English, and the episode about Baxter and the paint on a shoe is omitted, having already been told in the latter part of *Mike*.

First published March 17 1916 by D. Appleton and Company, New York, 326 pages. Bound in red cloth, lettered and decorated in gold with a frontispiece and seven illustrations by Clarence F. Underwood. This edition may be identified by the numeral "1" on the bottom of the last page of the text.

Characters

(1)   William FitzWilliam Delamere Chalmers, Lord Dawlish – 23 year old penniless young man who loves golf. Secretary to Brown's, an exclusive Club and is engaged to Claire.

(1)   Claire Fenwick – A touring company actress engaged to Lord Dawlish

(16)   Mr. Ira Nutcombe – Old American millionaire who was helped at golf by Lord Dawlish

(18)   Gates – A New York newspaperman friend of Lord Dawlish, now stationed in London as his paper's correspondent

(29)   Gerald Nichols – Lord Dawlish's friend of the law firm Nichols, Nichols, Nichols and Nichols

(31)   Percy Fenwick – Claire's 10 year old brother

(33)   Polly Davis – Claire's friend who married Lord Wetherby. An American ex-actress living in New York doing a barefoot dance at Riegelheimer's restaurant.

(34)   Algie Wetherby, Lord Wetherby – Poorest Earl in England who is an amateur painter

(36)   Roscoe Sherriff – Polly's press agent

(37)   Clarence – Polly's snake

(37)   Eustace – Polly's monkey

(38)   Dudley Pickering – Millionaire automobile manufacturer, middle-aged friend of Polly's who falls in love with Claire

(49)   Elizabeth Boyd – Heroine – Nutcombe's 21 year old niece who loves Lord Dawlish and rented Flack's Farm in Brockport, Long Island to raise bees

(54)   (Nutty) Claude Nutcombe Boyd – Elizabeth's brother

(57)   James – Elizabeth's cat

(73)   Daisy Leonard – One of Nutty's chorus-girl friends

(162)   Wrench – Polly's butler

Places

(9)   Brown's — An aristocratic and exclusive Club in St. James's
        Street, London
(23)   Pen and Ink Club — For Journalists and affiliated with the
        Players, in New York City

20a — UNEASY MONEY

First published October 4 1917 by Methuen & Co., London, 280
pages. Bound in light red cloth and lettered in black. First edition
stated on verso of title.

This differs slightly from the American edition.

21 – PICCADILLY JIM

First published February 24 1917 by Dodd, Mead and Company, New York, 364 pages. Bound in light orange cloth, lettered in black with a frontispiece and seven illustrations by May Wilson Preston. The only Wodehouse novel published by Dodd.

A partial sequel to *The Little Nugget*.

Characters

(1) Mr. Peter Pett — Millionaire financier bullied by his wife and loves baseball

(2) Mrs. Nesta Ford Pett — Mr. Pett's wife of two years in her early 40's who writes sensational fiction

(2) Willie Partridge — Mrs. Pett's nephew and brainless son of inventor Dwight Partridge who is working on an explosive

(3) Ogden Ford — 14 year old fat and precocious son of Nesta's

(8) Ann Chester — Heroine and Mr. Pett's niece with red-gold hair

(12) Jerry Mitchell — Mr. Pett's private physical instructor who loves Celestine

(16) (Jimmy) James Braithwaite Crocker — Hero and Nesta's 26 year old nephew and Bingley's son. Ex-journalist with the *Cronicle*. Talks like Psmith.

(17) Mrs. Eugenia Crocker — Nesta's sister and widow of millionaire G.G. Van Brunt who lives in London with her new husband

(19) Bingley Crocker — 50 year old obscure actor who married Eugenia five years ago

(26) Lord Wisbeach — Pseudonym for Gentleman Jack of Burke's gang who is an oily suitor to Ann

(27) Hammond Chester — Ann's father and Mr. Pett's brother-in-law

(28) Biggs — Pett's chauffeur

(29) Celestine — Mrs. Pett's maid whose real name is Maggie O'Toole

(31) Bud Smithers — Jerry's friend who owns a dog hospital on Long Island

(40) Bayliss — Mrs. Crocker's butler in London who likes Bingley and Jimmy

(159) Lora Delane Porter — Feminist writer friend of Nesta's

(170) Skinner — Bingley Crocker's alias as he buttles for the Petts

(175) Mary — The Pett's parlour-maid

(205) Aida — Mrs. Pett's pomeranian

(244) Mr. Sturgis — Proprietor of the International Detective Agency

(260)   Miss Trimble — A detective working for Mr. Sturgis

Places and Things

(9)   *At Dead of Night* — A novel by Nesta Ford Pett
(147)   Bachelor's Club — Jimmy is a member in London
(247)   *A Society Thug* — Another novel by Nesta
(271)   *The Lonely Heart* — Book of poetry written by Ann Chester

21a — PICCADILLY JIM

First published May, 1918 by Herbert Jenkins Limited, London, 316 pages. Bound in mustard yellow cloth, lettered in black. The first Wodehouse title to be published by this firm, who have with few exceptions remained his English publishers.

There are few minor changes in the text.

22 — THE MAN WITH TWO LEFT FEET

First published March 8 1917 by Methuen & Co., London, 298 pages. Bound in light red cloth and lettered in black.

Wodehouse's second short story collection for adults, with the first two stories taking top honors. Indeed, "Extricating Young Gussie" is generally overlooked, despite being the first in Wodehouse's most successful series featuring Bertie Wooster and Jeeves. In Jeeves' second and last recorded speech in this story ("Very good, sir, which suit will you wear?") is the germ of what was to become a constant fly in the ointment between servant and master, the question of the master's wearing apparel and personal adornment.

Bill The Bloodhound

Characters

Henry Pifield Rice — Young bumbling detective working for
    Stafford's International Investigation Bureau who loves Alice
Alice Weston — Chorus girl on tour in *The Girl From Brighton*
Walter Jelliffe — Comedian and star of *The Girl From Brighton*
Sidney Crane — Baritone and leading member of the cast
Miss Clarice Weaver — Female lead singer and an unpopular
    member of the cast

Extricating Young Gussie

Characters

Aunt Agatha Gregson — Bertie's aunt who is married to Spencer
    Gregson, a stock broker
Jeeves — Bertie's manservant
(Gussie) Augustus Mannering-Phipps — Bertie's cousin in New
    York engaged to Ray Denison
Bertie (Mannering-Phipps) — Narrator who is bossed by his
    Aunt Agatha
Julia Mannering-Phipps — Agatha's sister-in-law, Gussie's mother
    and widow of Cuthbert. Owns Beechwood in London and
    was once in vaudeville.
Ray Denison — Vaudeville singer engaged to Gussie
Abe Riesbitter — Vaudeville agent
George Wilson — Alias used by Gussie for the stage
Joe Danby — Ray's father, an old English vaudevillian in love
    with Julia

Things

"Fun in a Tea Shop" — Old vaudeville sketch done by Julia and Danby

Wilton's Holiday

Characters

Jack Wilton — Hero who spread a story at Marvis Bay about his tragic love affair
Spencer Clay — Young ass
Ellerton — Another young ass
Mary Campbell — Wilton's love
Amy — Imaginary girl of Wilton's who had died

Places

Bridley-in-the-Wold — Wilton's hometown

The Mixer — I — He Meets A Shy Gentleman

Characters

The Mixer — Bulldog terrier mutt born in an East End pub who narrates story
Shy Man — Bought The Mixer and burgled a house where Fred's father was caretaker
Fred — Barman at pub where Mixer was born

The Mixer — II — He Moves In Society

Characters

The Mixer — Bulldog terrier mutt narrates story
John the Chauffeur — Ran over The Mixer
Master Peter — 10 year old boy of wealthy parents
Peter's Nurse — Doesn't like The Mixer
Helen — Peter's mother
Peter's father — Owns prize-winning dog kennels
Jack — A dog belonging to Dick, the Groom
Toto — A toy dog belonging to a guest
Weeks — Butler

58

Crowned Heads

Characters

Katie Bennett — Heroine who works in a second-hand bookshop in New York owned by her grandfather

Genevieve — Katie's friend and cloak model at Macy's

Ted Brady — Hero who loves Katie and is champion high jumper and runner

Mr. Matthew Bennett — Katie's paralyzed old grandfather who imagines himself King of England

Mr. Murdoch — Mr. Bennett's friend and glazier

Mr. Schwartz — Mr. Bennett's friend and saloon-keeper

At Geisenheimer's

Characters

Miss Roxborough — Professional dancer at Geisenheimer's Dance Palace, married to Jack Tyson and narrates the story

Charlie Ferris — Tourist on his honeymoon who owns a drug-store in Ashley, Maine

Mrs. Mary Ferris — Charlie's wife who wins the Love-r-ly Silver Cup

Jack Tyson — Lives in Rodney, Maine

Izzy Baermann — Emcee at Geisenheimer's

The Making Of Mac's

Characters

Henry — Chief waiter at MacFarland's Restaurant in Soho, who came from the Guelph

Old Man MacFarland — Widower with a son and adopted daughter

Katie — Mac's adopted daughter and dancer in *The Rose Girl*

Andy MacFarland — Mac's son in love with Katie

Jules — Mac's cook originally from Paris

One Touch Of Nature

Characters

J. Wilmot Birdsey — American baseball fan living in London

59

Hugo Percy de Wynter Framlinghame — 6th Earl of Carrick-
steed — married Mae Elinor Birdsey

Mr. Waterall — Clean shaven baseball fan from New York living
in London as the correspondent for the *New York Chronicle*

Mr. Johnson — Alias John Benyon — Baseball fan who robbed
the New Asiatic Bank in New York

Black For Luck

Characters

Joseph/Reginald — One stray black cat adopted at different
times by Elizabeth and Boyd

Elizabeth Herrold — Struggling young writer

Francis — Janitor in apartment house

James Renshaw Boyd — Budding playwright who is heir to
Boyd's meat products

Paul Axworthy Briggs — Budding novelist in the apartment
house

The Romance Of An Ugly Policeman

Characters

Edward Plimmer — Police constable

Alf Brooks — Milkman

Ellen Brown — A cook loved by Plimmer who was going with
Alf

A Sea Of Troubles

Characters

Mr. Meggs — Chronic dyspeptic wealthy bachelor of 56

Jane Pillenger — Spinster and private secretary/typist to Mr.
Meggs

Constable Gooch — Police constable

The Man With Two Left Feet

Characters

Henry Wallace Mills — Voracious reader who is a paying cashier
at the New York Bank

Minnie Hall — Henry's wife who was a former dance instructress
Sidney Mercer — Formerly a paying cashier with Henry's firm,
    now a professional dancer at Geisenheimer's

22a – THE MAN WITH TWO LEFT FEET

First published in 1933 by A.L. Burt Company, New York, 284 pages. Bound in orange cloth and lettered in black. This is probably the most overlooked title in the Wodehouse bibliography. Burt was a reprint house and although Doubleday, Doran gave it permission to publish Doubleday had never itself issued this volume. Hence it becomes the first American edition and in addition contains three stories not in the English Edition.

The Man With Two Left Feet – see 22

Bill The Bloodhound – see 22

Extricating Young Gussie – see 22

At Geisenheimer's – see 22

The Making Of Mac's – see 22

One Touch of Nature – see 22

Black For Luck – see 22

The Romance Of An Ugly Policeman – see 22

A Sea Of Trouble – see 22

Absent Treatment

Characters

Reggie Pepper – A drone who inherited money from his Uncle Edward, a Collier. Narrator.
Bobbie Cardew – Fellow drone with a horrible memory
Mary Anthony – Hospital nurse with red-gold hair who married Bobbie

Rallying Round Old George

Characters

Reggie Pepper – Narrator and forerunner of Bertie Wooster

George Lattaker — Reggie's friend posing as Alfred, his non-existant twin brother

Harold Voules — Reggie's valet who was engaged to Pilbeam

Mrs. Vanderley — Stella's mother

Stella Vanderley — Engaged to George

Emma Pilbeam — Mrs. Vanderley's maid

Uncle Augustus Arbutt — George's uncle who gambled away his trust fund

Mr. Marshall — Owner of the yacht *Circe* which carried the party to Monte Carlo

Prince of Saxburg-Liegnitz — Assaulted by muggers and saved by George

Denman Sturgis — Private investigator

Count Fritz von Coslin — Equerry to the Prince

Doing Clarence A Bit Of Good

Characters

Reggie Pepper — Narrator who loved Elizabeth and was engaged to her

Elizabeth Schoolbred Yeardsley — Clarence's wife who wants Reggie to steal *The Venus*

Bill Schoolbred — Reggie's chum at Oxford

Clarence Yeardsley — An artist who married Elizabeth

Mr. Mathew Yeardsley — Clarence's father and an amateur painter who gave his picture, *The Venus,* to Clarence and Elizabeth but wants it back

23 – MY MAN JEEVES

First published in May, 1919 by George Newnes, Limited, London, 256 pages. Bound in light red cloth and lettered in black. Published in Newnes' 1/9d novel series, printed by Butler and Tanner.

Only four of the eight stories are about Jeeves. They were slightly altered when republished in *Carry On, Jeeves.*

Leave It To Jeeves

Characters

Bertie Wooster — Narrator visiting New York City and bothered by suits

Jeeves — Bertie's valet whose taste in clothes is infallible. He was once in the service of the financier Digby Thistleton, now Lord Bridgnorth.

Monty Byng — Bertie's friend who had a checkered suit admired by Bertie

(Corky) Bruce Corcoran — Bertie's friend who wants to be a portrait painter but turns into a comicstrip artist

Alexander Worple — Corky's rich 51 year old uncle in the jute business whose hobby is ornithology

Muriel Singer — Corky's fiancee who is a chorus girl and finally marries Worple

Sam Patterson — Impecunious author who ghosts a children's book of birds

Jeeves And The Unbidden Guest

Characters

Bertie Wooster — Narrator who has to keep Wilmot in his apartment for a month

Jeeves — Dislikes Bertie's cloth-topped boots, a pink tie and his Country Gentleman Hat

Lady Malvern — Aunt Agatha's friend who writes about society and conditions in prisons in America

Wilmot, Lord Pershore — 23 year old son of Lady Malvern who lives a sheltered life in Much Middlefold, Shropshire. Lives it up a bit too freely in New York and spends some time in jail

64

Rollo — Wilmot's newly acquired bull-terrier
Rocky Todd — Bertie's friend on Long Island (see *The Aunt And The Sluggard*)

Jeeves And The Hard Boiled Egg

Characters

Bertie Wooster — Narrator
Jeeves — Objects to Bertie's moustache. Has an aunt who paid for a movie star to visit her home.
(Bicky) Francis Bickersteth — Impecunious English youth to whom Bertie lends his apartment
Duke of Chiswick — Bicky's wealthy uncle

Absent Treatment — — see 22a

Helping Freddie

Characters

Reggie Pepper — Narrator who goes to Marvis Bay, Dorsetshire
Freddie Meadowes — Reggie's friend who loves Angela
Jimmy Pinkerton — Reggie's playwright friend who gets Tootles to say "Kiss Freddie" to Angela
Angela West — Engaged to Freddie
Tootles Medwin — Little boy whose parents have the mumps

Rallying Round Old George — see 22a

Doing Clarence A Bit Of Good — see 22a

The Aunt And The Sluggard

Characters

Bertie Wooster — Narrator
Jeeves — Has an aunt who likes riding in cabs. Writes all about New York City's night life for Rocky to send to his aunt.
Rockmetteller Todd — Poet friend of Bertie's who lives a quiet life on Long Island and hates New York City
Isabel Rockmetteller — Rocky's wealthy aunt who wants to live it up vicariously but learns her lesson from Jeeves
Jimmy Mundy — A reformer whose lecture cures Rocky's aunt

First published in 1919 by Boni and Liveright, New York, 284 pages. Bound in grey-blue cloth and lettered in white. The only Wodehouse title published by this firm.

Originally appeared in *Munsey's Magazine* as a serial in 1914, the plot provided by the editor, Bob Davis. George H. Doran is supposed to have reprinted the work in 1924 under the title *White Hope*, but no copy is known.

Characters

(9)   Mrs. Lora Delane Porter — Strong, firm, unpleasant author on Eugenics. A suffragette, atavist and physical fitness nut.

(10)   Ruth Bannister — Niece and disciple of Lora. Strongly determined, tall, healthy, dark-haired daughter of millionaire John Bannister who marries Kirk.

(10)   Bailey Bannister — Ruth's 27 year old brother who is an old-maidish busybody and dislikes his Aunt Lora. Junior member of the Wall Street firm of Bannister & Son.

(11)   George Pennicut — Kirk's English odd job man who has ginger hair

(11)   Kirk Winfield — 26 year old large and well-built artist with a medium private income

(32)   Percy Shanklyn — Kirk's English actor friend who is chronically "between jobs"

(32)   Hank Jardine — Kirk's childhood friend who is a prospector

(32)   Steve Dingle — Hank's 28 year old prize-fighting friend. Also Kirk's friend who becomes John and Bailey Bannister's gym instructor. In love with Mamie.

(48)   John Bannister — Ruth and Bailey's father who is head of Bannister & Son

(103) William Bannister Winfield — Ruth and Kirk's son — The White Hope

(107) Keggs — John Bannister's English butler

(114) Mamie — 19 year old Nurse who likes Steve

(117) Whiskers — Bill's Irish Terrier given by Hank

(127) Sybil Wilbur — Married Bailey

(172) Basil Milbank — A social butterfly who toyed with Ruth's affections

(184) Robert Dwight Penway — Kirk's artist friend who is an alcoholic

Books by Mrs. Porter

(11)   *The Dawn of Better Things*
(11)   *Principles of Selection*
(11)   *What of Tomorrow?*

24a – THE COMING OF BILL

First published July 1 1920 by Herbert Jenkins, London, 256 pages. Bound in red cloth and lettered in black. Text identical with number 24.

25 – A DAMSEL IN DISTRESS

First published October 4 1919 by George H. Doran, New York, 302 pages. Bound in brown cloth, lettered and decorated on front and back covers in black and orange.

The first of 39 titles published over 33 years. The first Wodehouse work with a slight theatrical background. (At the time the novel was written Wodehouse was at the height of his theatrical activity, having written and collaborated on 5 shows appearing on Broadway simultaneously – a feat never since eclipsed by another writer.) With Ian Hay, Wodehouse wrote a play based on *A Damsel in Distress,* produced in London in 1928. Keggs, first met in number 18, "The Good Angel," as a butler running matrimonial sweepstakes, appears in this novel doing the same thing.

Characters

(9)   John, Lord Marshmoreton – 48 year old widower with two children. Loves gardening and is half-heartedly writing the family history.

(9)   Percy Wilbraham Marsh – Lord Belpher (Boots), 21 year old son of the Earl attending Oxford

(9)   Lady Patricia Maud Marsh – 20 year old daughter of the Earl who was in love with Geoffrey but falls in love with George

(9)   Lady Caroline Byng – The Earl's sister and widow of Clifford Byng, wealthy colliery owner, who has Reginald, a step-son, whom she wants Maud to marry

(10)   Reginald Byng – Good-natured drone who loves Alice and marries her

(10)   Keggs – Butler at Belpher who runs a contest to see who marries whom

(10)   Albert – Page boy at Belpher who wants to be a butcher and resists the education foisted on him by Maud

(13)   Alice Faraday – Pretty and clever secretary to the Earl who finally elopes with Reggie

(17)   MacPherson – Gardener at Belpher Castle

(25)   Geoffrey Raymond – American nephew and secretary to millionaire Wilbur Raymond

(26)   Mac – Stage doorman at the Regal Theatre

(27)   George Bevan – 27 year old hero and alumnus of Harvard who loves golf and composes the music to hit musicals

(30)   Billie Dore — Golden-haired, cheerful and vivacious chorus girl
        from Indiana who loves flowers and finally marries the Earl
(32)   Babe Sinclair — American chorus girl in Bevan's musical comedy
(32)   Spencer Gray — Fat young man toying with Babe's affections.
        Alias used by Geoffrey Raymond
(113)   Rogers — Chauffeur at Belpher Castle
(137)   Mrs. Digby — Housekeeper at Belpher Castle
(173)   The Reverend Cyril Ferguson — Curate at Little Weeting who
        locks Percy in a closet

Places and Things

(9)   Belpher Castle — Hampshire estate owned by the Earl of
        Marshmoreton
(10)   Farmers' & Merchants' Bank — High Street in Belpher village
(11)   Athenaeum Club — Lord Marshmoreton is a member
(36)   In and Out Club — Social club in London
(87)   Marshmoreton Arms — Inn where George stayed in Belpher
(87)   Blue Boar — Pub with no overnight accommodations in Belpher
(136)   *Belpher Intelligencer and Farmers' Guide* — Local newspaper
(136)   Popgood, Grooly & Co. — Publishers of *Roses Red and Roses
        White* by Emily Ann Mackintosh
(171)   Moresby-in-the-Vale — Village near to Belpher
(171)   Little Weeting — Village near Belpher
(176)   The Three Pigeons — Pub in Little Weeting
(283)   Ye Cosy Nooke — Tea shop in Bond Street, London

25a — A DAMSEL IN DISTRESS

First published October 17 1919 by Herbert Jenkins, London, 320
pages. Bound in dark red cloth and lettered in black. A few minor
changes in the text of number 25.

26 – THE LITTLE WARRIOR

First published October 11 1920 by George H. Doran, New York, 384 pages. Bound in tan cloth, lettered in green and tan.

Characters

(7)	Freddie Rooke — Wealthy, kind and idle young drone who was a childhood friend of Wally and Jill's. Was Sir Derek's fag at Winchester. Loves Nelly Bryant.
(7)	Horace Parker — Freddie's valet in the Jeeves pattern
(8)	Sir Derek Underhill — 30 year old Member of Parliament who is engaged to Jill. Dominated by his mother and has a weak character.
(9)	Jill Mariner — English-American heroine who has pale gold hair and is loved by Wally
(9)	Lady Underhill — Derek's mother who dislikes Jill and is disliked by Freddie
(13)	Major Christopher Selby — Jill's lovable but scoundrelly uncle who is very like Ukridge. He loses Jill's fortune, goes to America and sells Nervino. Woos Mrs. Peagrim.
(17)	Ronny Devereux — Freddie's pal
(17)	Algy Martyn— Freddie's pal and member of the Drones Club
(19)	Ferris — Lady Underhill's maid
(33)	Wally Mason — Hero and childhood friend of Freddie and Jill's who is in love with Jill. Wrote the unsuccessful drama *Tried by Fire* under the pen-name of John Grant, but a successful writer of musical comedies with George Bevan. Does Swedish exercises in the morning.
(40)	Ellen Parker — Horace's wife and Freddie's cook
(84)	Nelly Bryant — American chorus girl stranded in London. Cast in *The Rose of America* in New York. Owns the parrot Bill and loves Freddie whom she eventually marries.
(84)	Bill — Nelly's parrot
(132)	Elmer Mariner — Jill's stingy farmer uncle in Brookport, Long Island
(139)	Julia Mariner — Jill's aunt
(139)	Tibby Mariner — Elmer and Julia's 8 year old child
(140)	Rover — Tibby's spaniel
(171)	(Ike) Issac Goble — Partner in Goble & Cohn, theatrical managers. Producing *The Rose of America*.

(183)	Otis Pilkington — Young, rich, spoiled author and lyrist of *The Rose of America* in New York who is dominated by his aunt, Olive Peagrim
(183)	Roland Trevis — Young composer of *The Rose of America*
(183)	Mrs. Waddesleigh (Olive) Peagrim — Otis' wealthy aunt who falls under Uncle Chris' spell
(188)	Mr. Saltzburg — Musical director of Otis' show who is also a frustrated composer
(189)	Babe — Redheaded chorus girl in Otis' show
(191)	(The Cherub) Mae D'Arcy — Chorus girl with condescending airs
(198)	Johnson Miller — Famous deaf choreographer for the show
(267)	Wentworth Hill — Famous English actor who gets fired from the show

Places and Things

(43)	*Tried by Fire* — Verse drama written by Wally Mason
(147)	Drones Club — Algy Martyn is a member
(149)	Bachelors Club — Freddie Rooke is a member
(181)	*The Rose of America* — Musical fantasy by Otis Pilkington and Roland Trevis, doctored by Wally Mason
(217)	Nervino — A patent medicine sold by Major Selby
(217)	Hotel Cosmopolis — Has expensive restaurant frequented by Freddie, Wally and Jill
(264)	*Follow the Girl* — A former hit musical comedy with book and lyrics written by Wally Mason

26a — JILL THE RECKLESS

First published July 4 1921 by Herbert Jenkins, London, 320 pages. Bound in blue cloth, lettered in black. The list of Wodehouse titles on the verso of the half-title page must be six in number, the last being *Indiscretions Of Archie*, costing 7/6d. The Mayflower Press printed this edition.

The test is the same as the above except that Freddie's valet here is named Horace Barker.

27 – INDISCRETIONS OF ARCHIE

First published February 14 1921 by Herbert Jenkins, London, 320 pages. Bound in light blue cloth and lettered in dark blue. The list of Wodehouse titles on the verso of the half-title page must be six in number, ending with *A Gentleman of Leisure*.

Not a novel, but a series of interconnected short stories.

Characters

(Archie) Archibald Tracy Moffam – Hero – Popular young English drone who is broke and married to Lucille Brewster

Daniel Brewster – Millionaire owner of the luxury Hotel Cosmopolis in New York City and Lucille's father. A connoisseur and art collector.

Lucille Brewster Moffam – Archie's wife who is small and has dark hair

Professor Binstead – Brewster's friend who specializes in art

Herbert Parker – Brewster's valet who gets fired

Mawson – Brewster's art dealer

James B. Wheeler – Popular young illustrator who has Archie pose for a magazine cover

Reggie van Tuyl – Archie's millionaire friend who gets engaged to Mabel Winchester

Officer Tim Cassidy – New York Policeman

Officer Donahue – New York Policeman

Roscoe Sherriff – Archie's press agent friend who gets him to hide a snake in the hotel

Mme. Brudowska – An actress who plays in tragedies

Peter – Mme. Brudowska's snake

General Mannister – Squiffy's uncle who is a member of the British Legation in Washington

(Squiffy) Lord Seacliff – Archie's alcoholic school chum

Bill Brewster – Lucille's brother who went to Yale

Salvatore – Archie's waiter at the Hotel

Vera Silverton – Extremely pretty actress starring in Benham's show

George Benham – Archie's playwright friend

Percy – Miss Silverton's bulldog

(Looney) Gus Biddle – Greatest left-handed pitcher of baseball

Mabel Winchester — English chorus girl engaged to Bill and Reggie
John Smith — The Sausage Chappie
Jno. Blake — English proprietor of a cigar store on 6th Avenue
Mrs. Cora Bates McCall — Lecturer on Rational Eating
Lindsey McCall — Cora's husband who's afraid of her
Washington McCall — Redheaded pie eating champion and 16 year old son of the McCall's
Wilson Hymack — Composer of "Mother's Knee"
Spectatia Huskisson — Singer whom Bill loves
Max Blumenthal — Music publisher
Aloysius Connolly — Brewster's friend and strike-making labor leader
Alice Wigmore — Painted the *Venus* and Wheeler's fiancee

Places and Things

Hotel Cosmopolis — Owned by Daniel Brewster
Pen and Ink Club — Wheeler is a member
Hermitage — Brewster's summer hotel
The Personality That Wins — Book which tried to help Bill talk to his father
"Mother's Knee" — Popular ballad that Archie helped to make famous

27a — INDISCRETIONS OF ARCHIE

First published July 15 1921 by George H. Doran, New York, 306 pages. Bound in light brown cloth, lettered and decorated in green.

28 – THE CLICKING OF CUTHBERT

First published February 3 1922 by Herbert Jenkins, London, 256 pages. Bound in green pictorial cloth, lettered and decorated in dark green. The list of titles on the verso of the half-title page must be eight in number, the last being *The Girl on the Boat*. There is a slight possibility that copies exist with seven titles only, ending with *Indiscretions of Archie,* but none are now known.

The first collection of The Oldest Member golf stories.

The Clicking Of Cuthbert

Characters

The Oldest Member – Pipe-smoking story teller who narrates this series
Young Man – Wanting to give up golf before hearing the story
J. Cuthbert Banks – Ardent young golfer in love with Adeline
(Aunt Emily) Mrs. Willoughby Smethurst – President of Wood Hills Literary and Debating Society who loathes golfers and brings culture to the area by way of guest lecturers
Adeline Smethurst – Emily's visiting niece who is loved by Devine and Banks
Raymond Parsloe Devine – Young novelist who is a member of the Literary Society. Loves Adeline.
Vladimir Brusiloff – Famous Russian novelist who lectured at Wood Hills and is a golfer who admires Cuthbert. Favorite authors are Wodehouse and Tolstoy.

Places and Things

Wood Hills – English suburb where story takes place
Flicker Film Company – California motion picture company who hires Devine

A Woman Is Only A Woman

Characters

The Oldest Member – Narrator
Peter Willard – Todd's golfing friend who is a poor player
James Todd – Willard's golfing friend who is a poor player

Grace Forrester — Loved by Willard and Todd until they find out she doesn't like golf

Freddie Woosley — Member of the golf club

Places

Woodhaven — Where story takes place

A Mixed Threesome

Characters

The Oldest Member — Narrator

The Young Man — To whom the Oldest Member relates this story

J. Mortimer Sturgis — 38 year old amiable fellow with private means who collected porcelain vases and took up golf to surprise Betty

Betty Weston — 25 year old friend of the Oldest Member engaged to Mortimer but loves Eddie

Eddie Denton — Mortimer's best friend who is an explorer and finally marries Betty

Sundered Hearts

Characters

The Oldest Member — Narrator continuing the story of Sturgis

The Young Man

Mortimer Sturgis — A 42 year old golfing fanatic

Mabel Somerset — Blue-eyed, golden haired girl who falls in love and marries Sturgis. Her cousin Mary is a Ladies Golf Champ while Mabel is Ladies Open Croquet champion.

The Salvation Of George Mackintosh

Characters

The Oldest Member — Narrator who plays a game with Celia and tells the story of a great talking golfer

The Young Man — To whom the story is told

Herbert Pobsley — Great talker while playing with the Young Man

George Mackintosh — Handsome young golfer who talked incessantly while playing. Loves Celia.

Celia Tennant — Loves George and hits him with a club to stop him from being an eloquent talker

Places and Things

Law firm: Peabody, Peabody, Peabody, Peabody, Cootes, Toots, and Peabody — to which George belonged

Ordeal By Golf

Characters

The Oldest Member — Narrator friend of Mr. Paterson who tells of losing temper at golf
Mitchell Holmes — Worked for Mr. Paterson and can imitate a bulldog fighting a Peke. Has a temper only while playing golf.
Millicent Boyd — Engaged to Mitchell
Alexander Paterson — President of Paterson Dyeing and Refining Company who has a treasurership opening in his company. Decides to have a game with Holmes and Dixon to see who gets it.
Rupert Dixon — Unpleasant rival to Holmes

Places

Marvis Bay Golf and Country Club — Where action takes place
(129) "The ideal golfer never loses his temper. When I played, I never lost my temper. Sometimes, it is true, I may, after missing a shot, have broken my club across my knees; but I did it in a calm and judicial spirit, because the club was obviously no good and I was going to get another one anyway."

The Long Hole

Characters

The Young Man
The Oldest Member — Narrates a story about a rule-book golfer
Ralph Bingham — Handsome golfing rival to Jukes and loves Amanda
Arthur Jukes — Handsome golfing rival to Bingham and loves Amanda
Amanda Trivett — Loved by Bingham and Jukes but already has a fiance

76

Rupert Bailey — Old friend of the Oldest Member who acts as judge with the Oldest Member for the contest

Places

Woodhaven, Leigh — Where action takes place

The Heel Of Achilles

Characters

The Young Man
The Oldest Member — Narrator of a story on the betting on golf. Alumnus of Cambridge and Jopp's secretary.
Vincent Jopp — American millionaire divorced three times and can do anything he puts his mind to
Amelia Merridew — Provisionally engaged to Jopp but loves another
Sandy McHoots — Winner of the British and American Open who taught Jopp
Mrs. Luella Mainprice Jopp — Former wife who talks babytalk to her Peke
Mrs. Jane Jukes Jopp — Former wife belonging to the horsey-sporting set
Mrs. Agnes Parsons Jopp — Former wife who is a hypochondriac

Places and Things

Wissahicky Glen — Golf club in Chicago
Flesho — Tonic for producing firm flesh used by G.K. Chesterton

The Rough Stuff

Characters

The Oldest Member — Narrates a story telling why women should take up golf while drinking a seltzer and lemon
The Young Man — Engaged to Genevieve
Ramsden Waters — Timid young golfer but forceful when actually playing it. Loves Eunice.
Eunice Bray — Beautiful woman who marries Ramsden
Wilberforce Bray — Eunice's younger brother
? — Eunice's aunt who collects dry seaweed

Marcella Bingley — Good golfer in competition with Ramsden and Eunice

George Perkins — Marcella's golfing partner

The Coming Of Gowf

Characters

King Merolchazzar of Oom — Learns to play golf

The Grand Vizier

High Priest of Hec — One of the 67 gods

Royal Gardener — Scotsman who teaches the King golf on the Linx

Ascobaruch — The King's half brother, a sinister man

28a – GOLF WITHOUT TEARS

First published May 28 1924 by George H. Doran, New York, 330 pages. Bound in green cloth, lettered in dark green. This edition must have the publisher's monogram beneath the copyright notice.

Differences from number 28 are slight, in the altering of place-names, golfers, shops from English to American. Other differences are as follows:

A Woman Is Only A Woman

Place

Manhooset — Scene of story

Ordeal By Golf

Place

Manhooset Golf and Country Club — Scene of story

The Long Hole

Characters

Rollo Bingham
Otis Jukes
Amelia Trivett

Place

Manhooset — Scene of story

The Heel of Achilles

Characters

The Oldest Member is an alumnus of Harvard
Flesho — Irvin Cobb uses it

29 – THREE MEN AND A MAID

First published April 26 1922 by George H. Doran, New York, 304 pages. Bound in brown cloth, lettered in dark brown on spine. This edition must have the publisher's monogram beneath the copyright notice.

Characters

(7) (Aunt Adeline) Mrs. Horace Hignett — Famous English writer on Theosophy lecturing in America. Bosses her son.

(9) Eustace Hignett — Weak, poetry writing son of Mrs. Hignett who owns Windles. Engaged to Billie and loves Jane.

(10) Sir Mallaby Marlowe — Mrs. Hignett's brother, an eminent lawyer

(10) Sam Marlowe — Hero — Sir Mallaby's 25 year old son who went to school and Oxford with his cousin Eustace. Plays tournament golf and loves Billie.

(17) Mr. Rufus Bennett — American millionaire head of Bennett, Mandelbaun and Co. who wants to rent Windles for the summer with his friend Mortimer

(17) Mr. Henry Mortimer — Rufus's friend who has a son, Bream

(18) Bream Mortimer — Looks like a parrot, grew up with Billie and wants to marry her

(23) (Billie) Wilhelmina Bennett — Heroine — Redheaded daughter of Rufus who was going to marry Eustace, but wants a Sir Galahad type and winds up with Sam. She loves golf, dogs and Tennyson.

(30) Pinky-Boodles — Billie's Peke

(34) J.B. Midgeley — Eustace and Sam's steward aboard the *Atlantic*

(77) Jane Hubbard — Billie's big-game hunting friend who loves Eustace

(148) Smith — Mortimer's bulldog

(153) John Peters — Sir Mallaby's clerk

(157) Miss Milliken — Sir Mallaby's secretary

(168) Montagu Webster — Mr. Bennett's English valet who is reminiscent of Jeeves

(228) Mrs. Withers — Cook at Windles

Places and Things

(8) *The Spreading Light* — Book by Mrs. Hignett

80

29a – THE GIRL ON THE BOAT

First published June 15 1922 by Herbert Jenkins, London, 320 pages. Bound in orange pictorial cloth, lettered and decorated in brown. This edition must list 8 titles on the verso of the half-title, the last being *The Clicking of Cuthbert*.

A beneficially revised work containing a preface, several added scenes, and a sub-plot not in the American version.

First published October 17 1922 by Herbert Jenkins, London, 320 pages. Bound in orange pictorial cloth, lettered and decorated in brown. This edition must list 9 titles on the verso of the half-title, the last being *The Girl on the Boat*. The publisher post-dated this book 1923 on the title page.

Uses theatrical background as in number 26 and the brother-sister routine as in number 24.

Characters

(9)   Sally Nicholas — 21 year old Heroine. A small, trim, brown-haired American who worked at a Dance Hall before inheriting $25,000.

(9)   Fillmore Nicholas — Pompous 25 year old brother who was expelled from Harvard. First becomes assistant stage manager of *The Primrose Way* and then its sole backer. Marries Gladys.

(9)   Augustus Bartlett — Sally's friend who works for the brokerage firm of Kahn, Morris & Brown

(10)   Elsa Doland — Sally's pretty actress friend with big eyes who marries Foster

(12)   Maxwell Faucitt — Oldtime English actor living in New York boarding house whose brother died leaving him a fortune and a fancy dress shop

(23)   Gerald Foster — Handsome Englishman in his mid-twenties engaged to Sally. Went to school with Ginger. An unsuccessful playwright who jilts Sally, and marries Elsa who leaves him.

(27)   Reginald Cracknell — The Millionaire Kid who was the original backer of *The Primrose Way*

(28)   Mabel Hobson — Chorus girl who talked Cracknell into giving her the starring role

(34)   (Ginger) Lancelot Kemp — Hero— Redheaded English chap who stopped a dog fight. Went to Cambridge and played Rugby. A dog lover who went to school with Foster and loves Sally. Finally marries Sally and owns dog kennels.

(59)   Bruce Carmyle — Ginger's wealthy cousin, a rising lawyer

(88)   Toto — Mrs. Meecham's dog

(94)   Gladys Winch — Bit-part actress engaged to Fillmore

(101) Mr. Bunbury — Producer of *The Primrose Way*

(207)   Bugs Butler — Unpleasant contender for the lightweight boxing title
(207)   Lew Lucas — Lightweight boxing champion
(209)   Lester Burrowes — Bugs' manager
(254)   Isadore Abrahams — Owner of the Flower Garden dance hall where Sally worked

Places and Things

(9)   Mrs. Meecham's Boarding House — Where Sally lived
(10)   Kahn, Morris and Brown — Wall Street firm where Bartlett works
(26)   *The Primrose Way* — Play by Jerry Foster which turns into a smash hit
(32)   Roville-sur-Mer — French seaside resort where Sally met Ginger
(186)   Laurette et Cie — Faucitt's dress shop in Regent Street
(196)   Monk's Crofton — The Carmyle home in Much Middleford, Shropshire
(269)   *The Wild Rose* — Unsuccessful play by Foster
(310)   Popp's Restaurant — An eatery in Pittsburgh owned and operated by Gladys and Fillmore

30a – MOSTLY SALLY

First published March 23 1923 by George H. Doran, New York, 318 pages. Bound in green cloth, lettered in dark red on spine. This edition must have the publisher's monogram beneath the copyright notice. Except for the title, identical with the English edition.

First published May 17 1923 by Herbert Jenkins, London, 256 pages. Bound in green pictorial cloth, lettered and decorated in dark green. This edition must list 10 titles on the verso of the half-title, ending with *The Clicking of Cuthbert*.

A short story collection featuring the greatest Wodehouse creations, Bertie Wooster and Jeeves. "The Great Sermon Handicap" was issued in the 1930s by Hodder and Stoughton singly in its series "Little Books of Laughter." This collection first introduces Bingo Little.

Titles in parentheses are the original magazine titles of the stories prior to book publication.

Jeeves Exerts The Old Cerebellum – No Wedding Bells For Bingo (Jeeves In The Springtime)

Characters

Bertie Wooster – Narrator who went to school with Bingo. Won a prize at his first school for the best collection of wild flowers.

Jeeves – Bertie's valet who has an aunt who loves the romantic novels of Rosie M. Banks

Bingo Little – Mortimer's nephew who loves Mabel. Tells his uncle that Bertie is really Rosie M. Banks.

Mabel – Waitress in a tea shop

Mortimer Little – Retired fat businessman who owned Little's Liniment – "It Limbers Up the Legs." He is a gourmet.

Jane Watson – Mortimer's cook engaged to Jeeves, but not for long

Things

Novels by Rosie M. Banks – *All For Love, A Red, Red Summer Rose, Madcap Myrtle, Only a Factory Girl,* and *The Courtship of Lord Strathmorlick*

Mauve shirts – Jeeves didn't think they suited Bertie

Aunt Agatha Speaks Her Mind — Pearls Mean Tears (Aunt Agatha Takes The Count)

Characters

Jeeves — Served Lord Frederick Ranelagh before coming to Bertie
Bertie Wooster
Agatha Gregson — Bertie's 5'9" aunt who heartily dislikes him
Aline Hemmingway — Girl crook Aunt Agatha wants Bertie to marry
(Soapy) Sidney Hemmingway — Aline's crook brother posing as a curate

Places and Things

Roville-sur-mer — Scene of story
Bright scarlet cummerbund — Jeeves objects to Bertie wearing it
Chipley-in-the-Glen — Village in Dorsetshire

The Pride Of The Woosters Is Wounded — The Hero's Reward (Scoring Off Jeeves)

Characters

Bertie Wooster — Gets ensnared with Honoria
Jeeves — On vacation
Bingo Little — Has a degree from Oxford, tutors Oswald and falls in love with Honoria and then with Daphne
Honoria Glossop — Large, brainy and dynamic girl who had attended Girton and wants to mould Bertie
Oswald Glossop — Honoria's horrible young brother
Aunt Agatha — Wants Bertie to marry Honoria
Lady Glossop — Honoria's mother
Daphne Braythwayt — Honoria's friend whom Bertie could like but with whom Bingo falls in love

Places and Things

Ditteredge Hall — The Glossop home in Hampshire
(61) "He clasped my hand silently, then chuckled like the last drop of water going down the waste-pipe in a bath."

Introducing Claude and Eustace — Sir Roderick Comes To Lunch (Sir Roderick Comes To Lunch)

Characters

Bertie Wooster — His uncle Henry was a looney. Engaged to
    Honoria but Sir Roderick breaks it off.
Jeeves — Put three cats and a fish in Bertie's bedroom
Aunt Agatha Gregson — Wants Bertie to marry Honoria and has
    them both to lunch. Dislikes Jeeves.
Spenser — Aunt Agatha's butler
Honoria Glossop — Loves literature, art galleries and concerts.
    Takes Bertie to them. Wants to get rid of Jeeves.
Sir Roderick — Honoria's father who is a nerve specialist and
    dislikes cats
Claude — Bertie's cousin, one of a twin
Eustace — Bertie's cousin, one of a twin
Aunt Emily — Henry's widow and Claude and Eustace's mother
(Dog Face) Lord Rainsby — Claude and Eustace's school chum
    at Oxford

Places

6A Crichton Mansions, Berkeley Street, W. – Bertie's London
    address

**A Letter of Introduction — Startling Dressiness of A Lift Attendent
(Jeeves and The Chump Cyril)** `

Characters

Bertie Wooster — Now in New York City
Jeeves — Detests Bertie's purple socks
Cyril Bassington-Bassington — Aunt Agatha foists him on Bertie,
    gets arrested and then gets cast into Caffyn's show
George Caffyn — Bertie's playwright friend who wrote *Ask Dad*
Blumenfeld — Manager of *Ask Dad*
Blumenfeld, Jr. — Causes Cyril to be fired from the cast

Comrade Bingo — Bingo Has A Bad Goodwood (Comrade Bingo)

Characters

Bertie Wooster

Jeeves

Lord Bittlesham — Bingo's uncle Mortimer who was made a peer. Member of Devonshire Club and owns the racehorse, Ocean Breeze.

(Bingo) Richard Little — Falls in love with Charlotte, gets a beard and joins the Heralds of the Red Dawn

Charlotte Corday Rowbotham — Member of the Heralds

Rowbotham — Charlotte's father and leader of the Heralds

Comrade Butt — Member of the Heralds in love with Charlotte

The Great Sermon Handicap

Characters

Bertie Wooster

Jeeves

Bingo — Tutoring Egbert Wickhammersley at Twing Hall and is in love with Cynthia

Lord Wickhammersley — Owner of Twing Hall and Bertie's father's friend

Claude and Eustace — Bertie's twin cousins reading with the Vicar at Twing

The Rev. Francis Heppenstall — Vicar at Twing who had tutored Bertie

Lady Cynthia Wickhammersley — The Earl's daughter and childhood pal of Bertie's. He was once in love with her.

James Bates — Heppenstall's nephew who is Assistant Master at Eton and engaged to Cynthia

Steggles — Studying with the twins and makes book on the length of the sermons given by the parsons in the neighborhood

The Rev. G. Hayward — Heppenstall's nephew

Brookfield — Heppenstall's butler and friend of Jeeves

Places and Things

Twing Hall — Twing, Gloscestershire, owned by Lord Wickhammersley

Nearby villages — Badgwick, Stapleton, Upper Bingley, Lower Bingley, Little Chickton-in-the Wold, Boustead Parva, Boustead Magna, Candle-by-the-Hill, and Fale-by-the-Water

The Purity of The Turf

Characters

Bertie Wooster
Jeeves
Bingo Little
Rupert Steggles
Claude and Eustace
Mrs. Penworthy — Twing's tobacconist's wife who won the Mother's Sack Race
Prudence Baxter — Head gardener's child who won the Girls' Open Egg & Spoon Race
Harold the Page Boy — Disqualified from the Choir Boys' Hundred Yard Handicap

The Metropolitan Touch

Characters

Bertie Wooster
Jeeves
Bingo Little — Falls in love with Mary and produces the Village School Christmas entertainment
Mary Burgess — The Rev. Heppenstall's niece
Brookfield — The Rev. Heppenstall's butler
The Rev. Herbert Wingham — Heppenstall's new curate and Bingo's rival. Engaged to Mary.
Wilfred Burgess — Mary's young brother
Squire Tressider — Squire of Twing

Places and Things

Twing Hall — Lord Wickhammersley's home
Cow and Horses — Pub in Twing
Twing Village Hall — Where the Christmas entertainment takes place
"What Ho, Twing!!" — A revue presented by Bingo at the Twing Village Hall

The Delayed Exit of Claude and Eustace

Characters

Bertie Wooster — Has an Uncle Clive in Worcestershire
Jeeves — Coolness with Bertie over his pair of Old Etonian Spats
Aunt Agatha
Claude and Eustace — Both fall in love with Marion
Marion Wardour — Bertie's actress friend
Uncle George — Bertie's uncle who's an alcoholic
Stevens — Uncle George's manservant

Bingo and The Little Woman — All's Well (Bingo and The Little Woman)

Characters

Bertie Wooster
Jeeves — Helps Bingo by telling Lord Bittlesham and Rosie that Bertie is not mentally stable
Bingo — Marries Rosie M. Banks, famous sentimental writer
Lord Bittlesham — Bingo's rich uncle who loves Rosie's novels
Rosie M. Banks — First posed as a waitress for a novel and married Bingo

Places and Things

Senior Liberal Club — Where Bingo first met Rosie who was a waitress
Drones Club — Bertie and Bingo are members
Novels by Rosie — *The Woman Who Braved All* and *Mervyn Keene, Clubman*

31a — JEEVES

First published September 28 1923 by George H. Doran, New York, 288 pages. Bound in light brown cloth, lettered in black. This edition must have the publisher's monogram beneath the copyright notice. Except for the title, identical with number 31.

32 – LEAVE IT TO PSMITH

First published November 30 1923 by Herbert Jenkins, London, 328 pages. Bound in green pictorial cloth, lettered and decorated in dark green. This edition must list 11 titles on the verso of the half-title, the last being *Love Among the Chickens*.

The second in the Blandings series and the last of Psmith. A highly diverting scene occurs with Baxter and the Flower Pots (pp 239-269).

Characters

(7)   Lord Emsworth — Fluffy-minded wealthy peer with excellent health who loves flowers

(8)   Hon. Freddie Threepwood — Lord Emsworth's younger son who loves movies and mystery novels and has a scheme to steal Aunt Connie's necklace. Wants to get into the bookie business and marry Eve.

(8)   Beach — Butler at Blandings who has trouble with his stomach

(9)   Angus McAllister — Head gardner at Blandings

(11)   Rupert Baxter — Spectacled, efficient secretary to Lord Emsworth whose former employer was the American millionaire, Horace Jevons. Finally gets the sack at Blandings and goes back to Jevons.

(12)   Lady Constance Keeble — Lord Emsworth's sister in her mid-40's who dominates both Lord Emsworth and her husband Joe

(12)   Ralston McTodd — Canadian poet whom Lord Emsworth offends at the Senior Conservative Club

(15)   Aileen Peavey – Young American poetress who is also known in the underworld as Smooth Lizzie. Loves Ed.

(16)   Eve Halliday — Tall, gay and slim school friend of Phyllis' who goes to Blandings to catalog its library and falls in love with Psmith

(18)   Joseph Keeble — Elderly husband of Lady Constance who amassed a fortune in South Africa

(21)   Phyllis Jackson — Joe Keeble's small and fragile step-daughter who married Mike Jackson

(38)   Ronald Eustace Psmith — Champion talker and school friend of Mike's. Left his uncle's fish business to start on his own. Loves and wins Eve. He believes in practical socialism and calls everyone "Comrade."

90

(40)   Mike Jackson — Formerly Psmith's father's estate agent. Currently a Master at a school while wanting to buy a farm in Lincolnshire. Married Phyllis.
(46)   Ada Clarkson — Ex-English mistress at Wayland House who taught Phyllis and Eve. Now runs an employment agency.
(46)   Jane — Phyllis' maid
(51)   Cynthia McTodd — Ralston's wife and school chum of Phyllis and Eve
(61)   Hon. Hugo Walderwick — Member of Drones Club whose umbrella Psmith takes to give to Eve
(121)   George Willard — Rose-growing friend and neighbor to Lord Emsworth
(141)   Susan — Lady detective named Simmons posing as a housemaid at Blandings who had been hired by Baxter
(174)   Edward Cootes — Young American professional card sharper who is in love with Aileen. Poses as Psmith's valet and wants to steal the Keeble necklace.
(221)   Jno. Banks — Hairdresser in the High Street at Market Blandings
(239)   Thomas — Footman at Blandings
(240)   Stokes — Footman at Blandings
(246)   Lord Bosham — Lord Emsworth's eldest son

Places and Things

(7)   Blandings Castle — Lord Emsworth's home in Shropshire
(8)   Vale of Blandings — On which the castle is situated
(34)   *Morning Globe* — Newspaper carrying Psmith's unusual advertisement
(38)   18 Wallingford Street, West Kensington — The Jackson flat
(46)   Wayland House — Phyllis and Eve's school
(59)   Drones Club — Located in Dover Street opposite Thorpe & Briscoe's. Psmith is a member.
(59)   Messrs. Thorpe & Briscoe — Coal merchants directly opposite the Drones Club
(60)   Ada Clarkson International Employment Bureau — At the top of Shaftsbury Avenue. Psmith goes there seeking employment.
(93)   Senior Conservative Club — The membership totals 6,111 including Lord Emsworth and Psmith
(126)   Market Blandings — Nearest town to the Castle (2 miles away)
(169)   Bridgeford — Neighboring town
(221)   The Emsworth Arms — Inn which serves the best beer in Market Blandings

(222) Bachelor's Club — Freddie Threepwood is a member
(242) Wragge's — Detective agency which employs Miss Simmons
(282) Shifley — The County Ball is being held in this village
(324) Much Middlefold — Psmith grew up in this village
(324) Corfby Hall — Home of the Smiths in Much Middlefold, Salop

32a — LEAVE IT TO PSMITH

First published March 14 1924 by George H. Doran, New York, 348 pages. Bound in blue cloth and lettered in black. Must have the publisher's monogram beneath the copyright notice. Identical with number 32.

33 — UKRIDGE

First published June 3 1924 by Herbert Jenkins, London, 256 pages. Bound in green cloth, lettered in dark green. This edition must list 13 titles on the verso of the half-title, the last being *Leave it to Psmith.*

Ukridge is personally Wodehouse's favorite character. Although other short story collections include Ukridge stories, this is the only collection solely devoted to him.

Ukridge's Dog College

Characters

Stanley Featherstonehaugh Ukridge — Wants to train his aunt's Pekes for the stage
Narrator — A writer who went to Cambridge and Ukridge's friend since school days
George Tupper — Was head of the same school Ukridge and narrator went to, and is now in the Foreign Office. Lends Ukridge money.
Aunt Julia — Ukridge's rich aunt who lives on Wimbledon Common
Bowles — Narrator's landlord who is an ex-butler
Gooch — Grocer in Sheep's Cray
Nickerson — Ukridge's landlord at The White Cottage

Places and Things

Ebury Street — Narrator lives in a flat here on the first floor
The White Cottage — Ukridge's Dog College in Sheep's Cray, Kent

Ukridge's Accident Syndicate

Characters

Ukridge — Uses Lunt's scheme to form an Accident Syndicate
Narrator — Ukridge's writer friend
Teddy Weeks — Ukridge's friend who is supposed to have an accident. Becomes famous actor who gets married.
Victor Beamish — Ukridge's friend who is a struggling illustrator
Bertram Fox — Ukridge's friend who is the author of "Ashes of Remorse" and other unproduced movie scenarios

93

Robert Dunhill — Ukridge's friend who works in the New
   Asiatic Bank
Freddie Lunt — Ukridge's friend who had an accident which
   started off the idea of the syndicate

Places

Bunch of Grapes — Pub in London

The Debut of Battling Billson

Characters

Narrator — 27 year old newspaperman
Ukridge — Manages Battling Billson
(Battling) Wilberforce Billson — Redheaded young boxer
Bowles
Flossie — Barmaid who loves Billson

Places

Coal Hole — Pub in London
White Hart — Inn at Barnes where Ukridge trains Billson

First Aid For Dora

Characters

Corcoran — Narrator who poses as a reporter from *Woman's
   Sphere*
Ukridge
Dora Mason — Secretary/Companion to Aunt Julia
Bowles — Formerly in the employ of the Earl of Oxted
Julia Ukridge — Ukridge's Aunt, a famous writer of romantic
   novels who has been elected President of the Pen & Ink Club
Muriel Watterson — Editress of *Woman's Sphere* and Aunt
   Julia's friend

Place

Heath House, Wimbledon Common — Aunt Julia's house in
   London

The Return of Battling Billson

Characters

James Corcoran — Narrator
Battling Billson — Saves Corky in London's East End and beats Alf Todd in a match
Flossie's mother
Ukridge
Cecil — Flossie's younger brother
Alf Todd — Boxing opponent in a contest with Billson

Ukridge Sees Her Through

Characters

(Corky) James Corcoran — Narrator
Ukridge
Dora Mason — Partner in the Norfolk Street Agency
Hank Phillbrick — Millionaire pal of Ukridge's from Canada
Aunt Julia — President of the Pen & Ink Club
Charlton Prout — Conceited young ass who is the Club's secretary
Mr. Biggs — Secretary of the Warner's Stores Social & Outing Club

Places and Things

Society — Magazine wanted Corky's account of the Pen & Ink Club dance
"Grey Myrtles" — Prout's book published by Dunstable

No Wedding Bells For Him

Characters

(Corky) James Corcoran — Writer for *Interesting Bits*
Ukridge — Used the alias "Mr. Smallweed" to a shop keeper to whom he owed money as "just an ordinary business precaution"
Frederick — Ukridge's pub friend who is a chauffeur
Mabel Price — Engaged to Ukridge but loves Ernie Finch
George Tupper
Bowles

Ernie Finch — Loves Mabel
Mr. Grindlay — One of Ukridge's creditors

Places

Balbriggan — The Price home in Peabody Road, Clapham
    Common

The Long Arm of Looney Coote

Characters

(Corky) James Corcoran — Attended Wrykyn
Ukridge — Also attended Wrykyn with Corky and part owner of
    Isaac O'Brien, 3 Blue St., St. James's — a bookie business
(Looney) J.G. Coote — Superstitious wealthy old Wrykynian
    chum of Ukridge's
(Boko) B.V. Lawlor – Another old boy, standing for Parliament
    at Redbridge
Herbert Huxtable — Opposing Boko for Parliament

Places and Things

Bull Hotel — Ukridge stayed here when in Redbridge
"Mother, She's Pinching My Leg" — Music-hall song written by
    Corky

The Exit of Battling Billson

Characters

Corky
Ukridge — Fights Thomas instead of Billson
Evan Jones — Travelling evangelist
Battling Billson
Lloyd Thomas — Ukridge's boxing opponent
Izzy Previn — Ukridge's partner in Isaac O'Brien who skips town

Places

Cap and Feathers — Pub where Billson trained in Wales

Ukridge Rounds A Nasty Corner

Characters

(Corky) James Corcoran — Hired to write the memoirs of Sir
   Rupert Lakenheath
Ukridge
Bowles
Elizabeth, Lady Lakenheath — Widow of Sir Rupert and Millie's
   aunt
Millie — Lady Elizabeth's niece who loves Ukridge
Leonard — Lady Elizabeth's parrot
Wassick — Aunt Julia's new secretary
Julia Ukridge

Places and Things

Peppo — It Bucks You Up — A patent medicine which Ukridge
   sells

33a – HE RATHER ENJOYED IT

First published March 19 1926 by George H. Doran, New York,
316 pages. Bound in red cloth, lettered in black. This edition must have
the publisher's monogram beneath the copyright notice. Identical with
Number 33.

34 – BILL THE CONQUEROR

First published November 14 1924 by Methuen & Co., London, 296 pages. Bound in red cloth, lettered in black. Has "First Published in 1924" on the verso of the title page.

Similar to number 16 where the hero rescues the girl in the water years before and the girl remembers him as the Sir Galahad type. Part of this plot was used for the Bolton-Wodehouse-Kern 1924 musical comedy, "Sitting Pretty." Judson and the Hat Stand (pp 244-247) ranks as a highlight of the more humorous moments.

Characters

(1)   Sir George Pyke — Forceful and fat founder/owner of the Mammoth Publishing Company. Widower of Lucy Maynard and has a son, Roderick.

(1)   Roderick Pyke — Tall, thin, intellectual who proposes to Flick but loves another

(1)   Percy Pillbeam — 23 year old snooper for Sir George and works on *Society Spice*. Has black hair plastered down and a thin moustache.

(3)   Frances Hammond — Sir George's strong and energetic sister who is the wife of Sinclair Hammond

(5)   Sinclair Hammond — 53 year old well-known archaeologist. Flick's uncle.

(8)   (Flick) Felicia Sheridan — Heroine with amber hair. 21 year old, very pretty and loves Bill West

(17)   Bob — The Hammond's Sealyham terrier

(17)   Cooley Paradene — Great millionaire friend of Sinclair's who is a rare book collector. Owns the Paradene Pulp & Paper Company. Wants to adopt Horace.

(17)   William Paradene West — Hero who is an alumnus of Harvard. 26 year old nephew of Cooley's who thinks he's in love with Alice but really loves Flick.

(21)   Judson Coker — Bill's childhood and best friend

(21)   Alice Coker — A beautiful girl, Judson's sister, whom Bill loves

(21)   Ridgway — Bill's valet

(22)   Roberts — Cooley's butler

(24)   Otis Paradene — Cooley's brother in real estate who sponges on him

(24)	Jasper Daly — Cooley's inventor brother-in-law who also sponges
(24)	Evelyn Paradene-Kirby — Cooley's niece in her mid-forties who talks baby-talk
(30)	J. Birdsey Coker — Alice and Judson's millionaire father
(43)	Horace French — In a gang of crooks. To be adopted by Cooley.
(44)	Professor Appleby — Crook who wants to steal Cooley's rare books by having Horace live with him. Believer in eugenics.
(55)	Wilfred Slingsby — Cooley's London Manager who steals his money to invest in theatrical enterprises
(83)	Toddy van Ritter — Judson's pal and member of the Fifth Avenue Silks
(97)	Wace — Hammond's butler at Holly House
(128)	Sherman Bastable — Horace's tutor
(131)	Joe the Dip — Member of the gang who wants to steal Cooley's books
(147)	Prudence Stryker — American chorus girl jilted by Wilfred who turns against him
(175)	Augustus Briggs — Sir George's chauffeur
(182)	Montague Grayson — Well-known writer of sunny novels

Places and Things

(1)	*Society Spice* — Magazine published by Mammoth
(1)	Mammoth Publishing Company — Owned by Sir George Pyke
(2)	Tilbury House — On Tilbury Street which houses the Mammoth Publishing Co.
(2)	Other Mammoth publications — *Pyke's Weekly, Daily Record, Sabbath Hour,* and *Tiny Tots*
(13)	Holly House — Where the Hammonds live in Wimbledon Common
(50)	Fifth Avenue Silks — A walking club of which Judson is the founding member
(65)	9, Marmont Mansions, Battersea – Flat shared by Bill and Judson
(226)	Antiquarian Club — Situated in Pall Mall. Cooley is a member.

34a – BILL THE CONQUEROR

First published February 20 1925 by George H. Doran, New York, 324 pages. Bound in yellow cloth, lettered in green. This edition must have the publisher's monogram beneath the copyright notice. Identical with number 34.

First published October 9 1925 by Herbert Jenkins, London, 256 pages. Bound in green pictorial cloth, lettered in black. This edition must list 13 titles on the verso of the half-title page, the last being The Coming of Bill.

The second short story collection about Bertie Wooster and Jeeves. Five of the ten stories previously appeared in number 23 and were substantially revised for this collection. "Fixing It for Freddie" was originally "Helping Freddie" and featured Reggie Pepper. "The Rummy Affair of Old Biffy" makes an uncommon use of one of Jeeves' relatives.

Jeeves Takes Charge

Characters

Bertie Wooster — Knows Lord Emsworth at Blandings and engaged to Florence

Jeeves — Formerly worked for Lord Worplesdon (Florence's father) who has an aunt who had taken Walkinshaw's Supreme Ointment for swollen limbs. Doesn't like Bertie's check suit.

Meadowes — Bertie's ex-valet who stole Bertie's silk socks

Lady Florence Craye — Bertie's fiancee. Imperious, serious girl who wants to improve Bertie's mind. Previously appeared in the not-yet collected Reggie Pepper story "Disentangling Old Duggie."

Uncle Willoughby — Bertie's uncle writing his *Recollections of a Long Life*

Oakshott — Uncle Willoughby's butler

Edwin — Florence's younger brother who is a boy scout

Places and Things

Easeby — Shropshire estate owned by Uncle Willoughby

Riggs and Ballinger — Uncle Willoughby's publishers

(25)   "It was one of those still evenings you get in the summer, when you can hear a snail clear its throat a mile away."

The Artistic Career of Corky — see 23

Jeeves and The Unbidden Guest — see 23

Jeeves and The Hard Boiled Egg — see 23

The Aunt and The Sluggard — see 23

The Rummy Affair of Old Biffy

Characters

Bertie — Whose relatives include an Uncle James and an Aunt
Emily who has a 6 year old son, Harold
Jeeves — Has a niece, Mabel
(Biffy) Charles Edward Biffen — Absentminded young Drone
who loves Mabel but forgets to meet her. Engaged to Honoria
Glossop but finally gets Mabel.
Mabel — Jeeves' niece who loves Biffy
Sir Roderick Glossop

Without The Option

Characters

Bertie — Gets arrested on Boat Race Night with Sippy. Pretends
to be Sippy when visiting the Pringles.
Jeeves
(Sippy) Oliver Randolph Sipperley — 25 year old impecunious
author who is supported by his Aunt Vera
Vera Sipperley — Imperious aunt of Sippy's who lives at Pad-
dock, Beckley-in-the-Moor in Yorkshire
Professor Pringle — Thin, balding, dyspeptic friend of Aunt
Vera's
Heloise Pringle — The Professor's daughter who looks like her
cousin, Honoria Glossop
Aunt Jane — 87 year old aunt of the Professor's who loves cats
Sir Roderick Glossop — Prof. Pringle's brother-in-law
Egbert — Jeeves' cousin and Constable of Beckley-in-the-Moor

Fixing It for Freddie

Characters

Bertie — Member of the Drones Club who has an Uncle Percy
Jeeves
Freddie Bullivant — Member of the Drones Club who woos and
wins Elizabeth

102

Elizabeth Vickers — Loved by Freddie
Tootles Kegworthy — Kid taken by Bertie who helps Freddie
    win Elizabeth

Things

Bailey's Granulated Breakfast Chips — Tootles likes them
Marvis Bay — Seaside resort in Dorsetshire

Clustering Round Young Bingo

Characters

Bertie — Writer of "What the Well-Dressed Man is Wearing"
    article for *Milady's Boudoir*
Jeeves — Takes exception to the soft silk shirts being worn for
    evening wear
Dahlia Travers — Bertie's kind aunt who owns *Milady's Boudoir*
Bingo Little
Rosie Little — Novelist Rosie M. Banks who has a marvelous
    cook wanted by Aunt Dahlia
Anatole — Superb French chef of the Little's
Thomas Travers — Bertie's uncle with bad digestion. Anatole is
    the only one who can cook for him.
George Travers — Bertie's other uncle suffering from bad
    digestion

Things

Milady's Boudoir — Woman's magazine run by Aunt Dahlia
Peabody and Simms — Shirt makers

Bertie Changes His Mind

Characters

Jeeves — Narrator for the first and last time. Used to be a page
    boy in a school for young girls and also worked for the well-
    known financier Montague-Todd.
Bertie — Has a sister, Mrs. Scholfield, in India with three
    daughters. Makes speech.
Peggy Mainwaring — 12 year old redheaded girl
Miss Tomlinson — Head of a girl's school

35a — CARRY ON, JEEVES

First published October 7 1927 by George H. Doran, New York, 316 pages. Bound in pictorial brown cloth, lettered and decorated in orange. This edition must have the publisher's monogram beneath the copyright notice. Identical with number 35.

First published October 15 1925 by Methuen & Co., London, 248 pages. Bound in red cloth, lettered in black. This edition has "First published in 1925" on the verso of the title page.

Characters

(1)	John B. Pynsent — Sam's millionaire uncle who is head of Pynsent Export & Import Company
(1)	Samuel Pynsent Shotter — Hero — Orphan who went to Wrykyn and loves Kay. Does physical culture exercises and writes the Aunt Ysobel column in *Pyke's Home Companion*
(3)	(Hash) Clarence Todhunter — Ex-cook of the tramp steamer *Araminter* who is engaged to Claire
(5)	Lord Tilbury — The former Sir George Pyke, owner of the Mammoth Publishing Company
(12)	Kay Derrick — Heroine — 22 year old golden-brown haired orphan living with her uncle, Matthew
(13)	Matthew Wrenn — Kay's uncle and editor of *Pyke's Home Companion*
(14)	Mr. Cornelius — Wrenn's good friend and House Agent for Valley Fields. Writing a history of Valley Fields.
(15)	Willoughby Braddock — Kay's childhood friend and Old Wrykinian who shared a study with Sam. Millionaire who has trouble with his housekeeper.
(16)	Mrs. Winnington-Bates — Kay's employer and mother of Claude
(17)	Claude Bates — Old Wrykinian and a worm who loves Kay
(18)	Mrs. Martha Lippett — Claire's mother and Willoughby's housekeeper
(19)	Claire Lippett — Wrenn's cook engaged to Hash
(63)	Edward Finglass — Dead crook who inhabited Mon Repos
(70)	Mrs. Frances Hammond — Lord Tilbury's sister
(87)	(Chimp) Alexander Twist — Owner of the Tilbury Detective Agency who uses the pseudonym, J. Sheringham Adair
(89)	(Dolly) Dora Gunn — Crook in her mid-twenties who married Soapy
(90)	(Soapy) Molloy — Crook who works with Chimp and uses the alias, Thomas G. Gunn
(112)	Sleddon — Willoughby's butler
(121)	Amy — Large, friendly dog

(150) Percy Pilbeam — Editor of *Society Spice*

(157) The Rev. Aubrey Jerningham — New vicar of Valley Fields

Places and Things

(1) Wilmot Building — On Upper Broadway in New York City where Pynsent has his office

(5) Mammoth Publishing Company — Owned by Lord Tilbury

(13) Valley Fields — A number 3 bus will take you to this S.E. 21 district of London. Corresponds to Wodehouse's favorite boyhood spot, Dulwich, where he went to school. This is the first of five novels to use this location.

(13) San Raphael, Burberry Road — Matthew Wrenn's house in Valley Fields

(13) *Pyke's Home Companion* — Mammoth publication edited by Wrenn

(14) Mon Repos — Next door to (semi-detached) San Raphael

(58) Matters and Cornelius — House Agents of Ogilvy Street in Valley Fields

(87) Other Mammoth Publications: *Tiny Folk, Sabbath Jottings, British Girlhood, Boys' Adventure Weekly*

(87) The Tilbury Detective Agency Ltd. — Owned and operated by Chimp Twist

(128) The Blue Anchor — Pub in Tulse Hill where Hash bought Amy

(150) *Society Spice* — Mammoth periodical

36a — SAM IN THE SUBURBS

First published November 6 1925 by George H. Doran, New York, 346 pages. Bound in green pictorial cloth, lettered in dark green. This edition must have the publisher's monogram beneath the copyright notice. With the exception of the title, identical with number 36.

106

First published April 15 1926 by Herbert Jenkins, London, 318 pages. Bound in green pictorial cloth, lettered in black. This edition must list 14 titles on the verso of the half-title page, the last being *The Coming of Bill.*

The second collection of golfing stories narrated by The Oldest Member.

The Heart of A Goof

Characters

Oldest Member — Narrator
Young Man
Ferdinand Dibble — A goof on golf who loves Barbara
Barbara Medway — Loves Ferdinand
George Parsloe — Ferdinand's golf rival at Marvis Bay

High Stakes

Characters

Oldest Member
Young Man
Bradbury Fisher — American millionaire who collects golf relics
Blizzard — Bradbury's butler who had previously been with an
    Earl for 15 years
J. Gladstone Bott — Rival collector who wants Blizzard
Evangeline Fisher — Bradbury's domineering wife, his fifth
Vosper — Ex-butler to the Duke of Bootle and now the Fisher
    butler

Places

Goldenville, Long Island — Scene of story

Keeping In With Vosper

Characters

Oldest Member
Young Man
Bradbury Fisher

Rupert Worple — Bradbury's jail friend
Evangeline Fisher
Mrs. Lora Smith Maplebury — Bradbury's mother-in-law
Hildebrand Vosper — Bradbury's English butler who had been
    with a Duke for 18 years
Alfred — Evangeline's airdale

Chester Forgets Himself

Characters

Oldest Member
Young Man
Chester Meredith — Loves Felicia
Felicia Blakeney — 23 year old beautiful friend of Jane's
Jane Waterfield
Wilmot Royce — Felicia's mother who wrote such novels as
    Sewers of The Soul, The Stench of Life and *Grey Mildew*
Crispin Blakeney — Felicia's brother whom Chester dislikes. He
    is a lecturer and essayist.

The Magic Plus Fours

Characters

Oldest Member
George William Pennefather — The Young Man to whom the
    Oldest Member narrates his stories
Nathaniel Frisby — Played and beat George in a game
Wallace Chesney — Rich, handsome and exceedingly modest
    fellow engaged to Charlotte who bought a pair of gaudy plus
    fours from the Cohen Bros.
Charlotte Dix — Engaged to Wallace
Raymond Gandle — An artist who belongs to the Golf Club
Peter Willard — Member of the Golf Club

The Awakening of Rollo Podmarsh

Characters

Oldest Member
Young Man
Rollo Podmarsh — 28 year old golfer who lives with his mother

Mrs. Podmarsh — Rollo's mother
Mary Kent — Daughter of Mrs. Podmarsh's friend who is loved
   by Rollo
Lettice Willoughby — Mrs. Podmarsh's granddaughter
Enid Willoughby — Rollo's sister and Lettice's mother

Rodney Fails To Qualify

Characters

Oldest Member
Secretary of Club
Jane Packard — Slow, romantic girl
William Bates — Powerful, ponderous and large fellow who loves
   Jane
Rodney Spelvin — Sleek poet who gets engaged to Jane but
   hates golf

Jane Gets Off The Fairway

Characters

Oldest Member
Secretary of the Club
William Bates — Married Jane and has her sent white violets
   every anniversary
Jane Bates — Romantic girl
Rodney Spelvin – Wrote the novel, *The Purple Fan*
Braid Vardon Bates — 4 year old son of William and Jane

Things

Book — *Wodehouse On The Niblick*
Florist — Jukes, Enderby and Miller

The Purification of Rodney Spelvin

Characters

Oldest Member
Secretary of the Club
William Bates
Jane Bates
Braid Vardon Bates

Rodney Spelvin — 33 year old poet-novelist who wants to learn golf

Anastatia Bates — William's sister who is an excellent golf teacher

Reginald Brown — Detective with the Quick Results Agency

Cyril Delancey — Detective with the Quick Results Agency

37a — DIVOTS

First published March 4 1927 by George H. Doran, New York, 316 pages. Bound in orange pictorial cloth, lettered in black. This edition must have the publisher's monogram beneath the copyright notice. With the exception of the title, identical with number 37.

First published April 28 1927 by Methuen & Co., London, 252 pages. Bound in blue cloth, lettered in black. This edition has "First Published in 1927" on the verso of the title page.

Characters

(1)   George Finch — Hero from East Gilead, Ohio, living at the Sheridan Apartment House in Greenwich Village. Small, slim and wealthy man who fancies himself an amateur artist.

(2)   Frederick Mullet — Finch's man of all work. Ex-crook who marries Fanny.

(2)   James Hamilton Beamish — Author in his early 30's of the famous Beamish Booklets who lives at the Sheridan. Efficiency expert who falls in love with May Stubbs.

(6)   Officer Garroway — Policeman wanting to become a poet, takes instruction from Beamish.

(13)   Fanny Welch — Mullett's fiancee who is a pickpocket

(19)   Molly Waddington — 20 year old heroine who is short and plump

(20)   Sigsbee Horatio Waddington — Molly's father who loves the west. An ex-millionaire who is browbeaten and dominated by his wealthy wife.

(25)   Mrs. Waddington — Molly's stepmother. Widow of P. Homer Horlick, the Cheese King.

(26)   Rupert Antony Ferris — Waddington's butler who used to work in Bragmarley Hall, Little-Seeping-in-the-Wold, Salop

(26)   Lord Hunstanton — Englishman who sponges on Mrs. Waddington

(63)   May Stubbs — Mrs. Waddington's palmist, using the alias Madame Eulalie. Comes from East Gilead who knew George there. Falls in love with Beamish.

(150)   Rev. Gideon Voules — Clergyman who should have married George and Molly

(168)   L. Lancelot Biffen — Editor-in-Chief of *Town Gossip,* who lives in the Sheridan

Places and Things

(1)   Sheridan Apartment House — Near Washington Square in New York City

(1)   Purple Chicken — Restaurant in the Sheridan which gets raided.

38a – THE SMALL BACHELOR

First published June 17 1927 by George H. Doran, New York, 318 pages. Bound in yellow pictorial cloth, lettered in brown. This edition must have the publisher's monogram beneath the copyright notice. Identical with number 38.

First published September 27 1927 by Herbert Jenkins, London, 320 pages. Bound in green cloth, lettered in black. Has "First Printing" and the year on the verso of the title page.

The first of three collections of Mr. Mulliner stories. He tells the tallest tales, on whatever subject comes up during the conversation at the Angler's Rest, having a nephew or niece whose experience exactly fits the topic.

The Truth About George

Characters

Mr. Mulliner — Short and stout middle-aged narrator with round and honest blue eyes

George Mulliner — Nephew who stuttered and loved crossword puzzles

Susan Blake — Vicar's slim, fair daughter who loves George

Places and Things

Angler's Rest — The bar-parlour in which Mr. Mulliner tells his tales

East Wobsley — Village where George and Susan live in Worcestershire

Little-Wigmarsh-in-the-Dell — Neighboring hamlet to East Wobsley

Higgleford-cum-Wortlebury-beneath-the-Hill — Another neighboring hamlet

Dog and Duck — Pub at Pondelbury Parva

Chatsworth — George's cottage in East Wobsley

Cow and Wheelbarrow — Pub in East Wobsley

A Slice of Life

Characters

Miss Postlethwaite — Courteous and efficient barmaid at the Angler's Rest who is a movie fan

Mr. Mulliner

Wilfred Mulliner — Mr. Mulliner's brother who invents cosmetics. Assumes the alias of Straker to win Angela's love.

Angela Purdue — Pretty, wealthy girl to whom Wilfred is engaged
Sir Jasper ffinch-ffarrowmere, Bart. — Angela's fat guardian
Murgatroyd — Sir Jasper's butler
Percival Mulliner — Angela and Wilfred's younger son
Ferdinand Mulliner — Angela and Wilfred's older son

Places and Things

Raven Gypsy Face Cream — Cosmetic invented by Wilfred
Snow of the Mountain Lotion — Another cosmetic invented by Wilfred
Senior Test-Tubes — Wilfred is a member of this chemist club in St. James's
ffinch Hall — Sir Jasper's home in Yorkshire
ffinch Arms — Inn
Ease-O — Good for lumbago
Mulliner's Reduc-O — Slimming preparation

Mulliner's Buck-U-Uppo

Characters

Mr. Mulliner
Augustine Mulliner — Nephew who is a shy, timid, pale young curate assisting Brandon. Loves Jane and becomes secretary to the Bishop.
(Pieface) The Rev. Stanley Brandon — Vicar of Lower Briskett-in-the-Midden with a violent temper. Had been a heavyweight boxer at Cambridge.
Jane Brandon — The Rev. Stanley's daughter in love with Augustine
(Boko) Bishop Bickerton — Stanley's bishop and old school chum
Mrs. Wardle — Augustine's landlady

Places and Things

Buck-U-Uppo — Wilfred's new tonic
The Gables — Angela and Wilfred's home in Lesser Lossingham, Salop

114

The Bishop's Move

Characters

Mr. Mulliner — Drinks a Scotch & Lemon
Augustine Mulliner
Bishop of Stortford — Augustine's boss
(Catsmeat) The Rev. Trevor Entwhistle — Headmaster of Harchester who is an old school chum of the Bishop's
(Fatty) **Lord Hemel of Hempstead** — Another old schoolmate of the Bishop's
General Sir Hector Bloodenough, V.C., K.C.I.E., M.V.O. — Chairman of the College Board of Governors

Places and Things

Angler's Rest
Steeple Mummery — Augustine's new vicarage
Harchester — Public school

Came The Dawn

Characters

Mr. Mulliner
Lancelot Bassington Mulliner — Nephew who wants to be a poet. Signed to a Hollywood contract.
Jeremiah Briggs — Lancelot's wealthy uncle who owns Briggs's Breakfast Pickles
Angela — The Earl's daughter whom Lancelot loves
The Earl of Biddlecombe — Impoverished Earl
Isadore Zinzinheimer — Head of the Bigger, Better & Brighter Motion Picture Company of Hollywood who signs up Lancelot
Slingsby Purvis — Lancelot's rival
Bewstridge — Jeremiah's butler
Fotheringay — Lord Biddlecombe's butler

Places and Things

Night Clubs — The Mauve Mouse, The Scarlet Centipede, The Vicious Cheese, The Gay Fritter, The Placid Prune, and The Ham and Beef
Junior Lipstick Club — Angela is a member
Villa Chutney, Putney — Where Jeremiah lives.

The Story of William

Characters

Miss Postlethwaite — Barmaid at the Anglers' Rest
Mr. Mulliner
William Mulliner — Mr. Mulliner's uncle
Myrtle Banks — Girl with whom William is in love
Desmond Franklyn — William's rival
John San Francisco Earthquake Mulliner — William and Myrtle's
  son

Portrait of A Disciplinarian

Characters

Mr. Mulliner
Frederick Mulliner — Nephew in love with Jane
Dr. George Mulliner — Freddie's brother
Nurse Wilks — Freddie and Jane's 85 year old Nannie
Jane Oliphant — Freddie's ex-fiancee who becomes re-engaged
  to him

Places

Bingley-on-Sea — Resort town where George has his practice
  and where Nurse Wilks lives
Wee Holme — Nurse Wilks' house

The Romance of A Bulb-Squeezer

Characters

Mr. Mulliner
Clarence Mulliner — Cousin who is a fashion photographer and
  loves Gladys
Jno. Horatio Biggs, O.B.E. — Mayor of Tooting East. An ugly
  fellow who wants Clarence to take his picture. Kidnaps
  Clarence to take his daughter's photo.
Meadows — The Mayor's butler
Gladys Biggs — Mayor's daughter in love with Clarence

Things

Negative and Solution Club — Clarence is a member of this
  photographer's club in Pall Mall

116

Honeysuckle Cottage

Characters

Mr. Mulliner
James Rodman — Distant cousin who is a mystery writer
Leila J. Pinckney — Sentimental novelist who was James' aunt
William — James' dog
Rose Maynard — Heroine out of a Pinckney novel who loves
    James
Doctor Brady — Local doctor
Andrew McKinnon — Partner in McKinnon and Gooch, Rod-
    man's literary agents
Col. Henry Carteret — Rose's guardian who loves her

Places and Things

Honeysuckle Cottage — Leila left her home to Rodman
Novels by Leila — *The Love Which Prevails, Scent O' the Blos-
    som, Heather O' the Hills* and *Rupert's Legacy*
Novel by Rodman — *The Secret Nine*
Prodder and Wiggs — Rodman's publishers
Bunch of Grapes — Pub owned by Jno. Biggs

39a — MEET MR. MULLINER

First published March 2 1928 by Doubleday, Doran & Co.,
Garden City, New York, 308 pages. Bound in orange-yellow cloth,
lettered in dark red. The first edition is so stated on the verso of the
title beneath the copyright notice. Identical with number 39.

40 – MONEY FOR NOTHING

First published July 27 1928 by Herbert Jenkins, London, 320 pages. Bound in orange cloth, lettered in black. "First Printing 1928" appears on the verso of the title page.

Introduces Hugo Carmody and Ronald Fish, met again in number 42. A highlight of humor is the episode of Hugo, Shakespeare, and the Burglar (pp 140-147).

Characters

(12)   Chas. Bywater – Chemist in Rudge and its chief gossip
(12)   Colonel Meredith Wyvern – Pat's father and estranged friend of Lester's
(14)   Lester Carmody – John's fat and wealthy uncle. Hugo's uncle and trustee. Miserly fellow who tries to burgle his own home.
(15)   Patricia Wyvern – Heroine – The Colonel's daughter
(17)   John Carroll – Hero – Lester's nephew who is the manager of his estate
(17)   Emily – John's Welch terrier who is partial to cough drops
(23)   Bolt – Lester's chauffeur
(25)   Hugo Carmody – Lester's nephew and John's cousin. An amiable drone who went to Eton and Trinity College, Cambridge and wants to run a nightclub with a friend.
(27)   (Chimp) Dr. Alexander Twist – A small, weedy crook running Healthward Ho
(29)   Egbert Flannery – An ex-sergeant-major who works at Healthward Ho
(37)   Ronald Overbury Fish – Hugo's school chum and amiable drone who wants to start a nightclub called The Hot Spot off Bond Street in London
(56)   (Soapy) Thomas G. Molloy – 42 year old American confidence man
(67)   Dolly Molloy – Pretty wife of Soapy's
(81)   The Rev. Alistair Pond-Pond – Vicar at Rudge
(138) Bessemer – Ronnie's valet
(168) Sturgis – Butler at Rudge Hall
(188) Constable Mould – Policeman in Rudge

118

(11)   Rudge-in-the-Vale, Worcester — Village of 3,541 with a Norman
         church and eleven pubs
(11)   Carmody Arms — Pub in Rudge-in-the-Vale
(11)   The River Skirme — Flows along Rudge
(12)   Brophy's Paramount Elixir — Said to be good for gnat-bites
(12)   Rudge Hall — Seat of the Carmody family
(25)   Healthward Ho — Physical culture establishment just outside
         Lowick in Worcestershire
(37)   The Hot Spot — Nightclub run by Ronnie and Hugo
(48)   The Mustard Spoon — Nightclub in London
(88)   Plough and Chicken — Pub in Rudge
(88)   Bunch of Grapes — Pub in Rudge
(88)   Waggoner's Rest — Pub in Rudge

40a — MONEY FOR NOTHING

First published September 28 1928 by Doubleday, Doran, Garden City, New York, 336 pages. Bound in blue pictorial cloth, lettered in orange. The first edition is so stated beneath the copyright notice. Identical with number 40.

First published April 30 1929 by Herbert Jenkins, London, 320 pages. Bound in orange cloth, lettered in black, with "First Printing 1929" on the verso of the title page.

The second collection of short stories all about Mr. Mulliner.

The Reverent Wooing of Archibald

Characters

Mr. Mulliner's Drinking Companions: Gin-and-Ginger-Ale, Draught Stout, Small Bass, and the Double Whisky-and-Splash

Mr. Mulliner — Drinks hot Scotch and lemon

Archibald Mulliner — Intelligent and wealthy nephew who loves Aurelia. Does a wonderful imitation of a hen laying an egg. Member of the Drones Club.

Aurelia Cammarleigh — Superbly handsome tall girl who gives a haughty impression but is really one of the girls

Meadowes — Archie's valet

Algy Wymondham-Wymondham — Member of the Drones Club

Lysander — Aurelia's bulldog who snores

Places and Things

Brawstead Towers — Aurelia's aunt's country house in Sussex

Junior Lipstick — Club for the modern girl

The Man Who Gave Up Smoking

Characters

Mr. Mulliner's Drinking Companions: Lemon Squash, and Tankard-of-Ale

Mr. Mulliner

Ignatius Mulliner — Nephew who plays the ukulele and paints portraits. Gives up smoking to please Hermione whom he loves

Hermione Rossiter — Beautiful daughter of Herbert who wants to be loved for her brains

Cyprian Rossiter — Hermione's tall, thin brother who writes art criticism

George Rossiter — Stout, pink brother who is a loafer and sponger.

Places and Things

Goat and Bottle — Pub in the Fulham Road, London

The Story of Cedric

Characters

Mr. Mulliner

Miss Postlethwaite — Barmaid who broke her engagement to Alfred Lukyn for wearing yellow shoes

Cedric Mulliner — Cousin who is a neat, prim, fussy and fat 45 year old snob

Myrtle Watling — Calm, strong secretary to Cedric. Lives in Valley Fields and loves him.

Lady Chloe Downblotton — Engaged to Claude and daughter of the 7th Earl of Choole

Claude — Artist engaged to Lady Chloe who wore yellow shoes with dress clothes and borrowed Cedric's correct shoes, leaving Cedric with his

Mortal Error — Myrtle's cat

Places

7, Nasturtium Villas, Marigold Road — Myrtle's house in Valley Fields

The Ordeal of Osbert Mulliner

Characters

Mr. Mulliner

Miss Postlethwaite

Osbert Mulliner — Rich nephew who collects jade. Loves Mabel.

Mabel Petherick-Soames — Loves Osbert

J. Bashford Braddock — Mabel's cousin and explorer who loves her

Parker — Osbert's valet

Major-General Sir Masterman Petherick-Soames — Mabel's uncle

Ernest and Harold — Burglars in Osbert's house

Places and Things

Drones Club — Captain J.G. Walkinshaw is a member
Junior Bird-Fanciers — Club in London
United Jade-Collectors — Club of which Osbert is a member
Peabody, Thrupp, Thrupp, Thrupp, Thrupp and Peabody — Osbert's lawyers
Cohen Bros. — Second-hand clothing firm near Covent Gardens

Unpleasantness at Bludleigh Court

Characters

Mr. Mulliner
Charlotte Mulliner — Niece who is a poet and writes "Vignettes in Verse." Loves Aubrey.
Aubrey Bassinger — Loves Charlotte and writes "Pastels in Prose" under the name of Trefusis
Colonel Sir Francis Pashley-Drake — Big game hunter who is Aubrey's uncle
Sir Alexander Bassinger — Aubrey's father, a sportsman
Reginald Bassinger — Aubrey's older brother
Wilfred Bassinger — Aubrey's younger brother

Places and Things

The Crushed Pansy — The Restaurant with a Soul
Bludleigh Court — Aubrey's home in Lesser Bludleigh, Goresby-on-the-Ouse, Bedfordshire
Animal-Lovers Gazette — Magazine which rejects Charlotte's "Vignette"

Those In Peril On The Tee

Characters

Mr. Mulliner — Narrates this golf story. Should properly belong to the Oldest Member who tells other stories regarding Agnes Flack and Sidney McMurdo.
Miss Postlethwaite
Agnes Flack — Daughter of a distant cousin. Amazon and golf champion.
Sidney McMurdo — Beefy dumb golfer who becomes engaged to Agnes

Frederick Pilcher — Artist who loves Agnes

John Gooch — Writer of detective stories who loves Agnes

Things

The Mystery of the Severed Ear — Novel by John Gooch

Something Squishy

Characters

Mr. Mulliner

Lady Wickham — Cousin who writes novels

Roberta Wickham — Lady Wickham's beautiful daughter who plays practical jokes. Red-head.

Mild-and-Bitter — Mr. Mulliner's companion

Roland Moresby Attwater — Essayist and literary critic who loves Bobbie and gets engaged to Lucy

Lucy Moresby — Sir Joseph's adopted daughter who loves Roland

Sir Joseph Moresby — Roland's uncle who is a metropolitan magistrate

Bryce — Roland's valet

Sidney — Roland's sanke

Sir Claude Lynn — House guest at Skeldings who proposed to Roberta

Simmons — Lady Wickham's butler

Places and Things

Skeldings Hall — Lady Wickham's estate in Hertfordshire

Blenkinsop's — Publishers of Roland's book

The Awful Gladness of The Mater

Characters

Mr. Mulliner

Dudley Finch — Roland's cousin who loves Roberta

Roberta Wickham — Redheaded daughter of Mr. Mulliner's cousin

Sampson Broadhurst — Dudley's Australian godfather who offered to teach Dudley sheep farming

Roland Attwater — Engaged to Lucy Moresby

Simmons — Lady Wickham's butler

Lady Wickham — Roberta's mother who writes novels under the name of George Masterman

Places and Things

Drones Club — Dudley is a member
Wickham Arms — Inn near Skeldings Hall
Skeldings Hall — Lady Wickham's residence

The Passing of Ambrose

Characters

(Algy) Algernon P. Crufts — Ambrose's friend who introduced
 him to Bobbie. Next door neighbor.
Ambrose Wiffin — Algy's friend who loves Bobbie
Mr. Mulliner
Wilfred — Bobbie's small cousin
Esmond Bates — Wilfred's friend
(Bobbie) Roberta Wickham — Loved by Ambrose

Things

Drones Club — Algy and Ambrose are members of the club
 located in Dover Street

41a — MR. MULLINER SPEAKING

First published February 21 1930 by Doubleday Doran, Garden
City, New York, 334 pages. Bound in blue pictorial cloth, lettered
in dark blue. The first edition is so stated beneath the copyright notice.
Identical with number 41.

First published July 1 1929 by Doubleday Doran, Garden City, New York, 328 pages. Bound in dark brown cloth, lettered in yellow. The first edition is so stated beneath the copyright notice.

This is the third novel in the Blandings series and deals humorously with the kidnapping of the Empress. A high spot is The Fight at Mario's (pp 112-118).

Characters

(1)	Beach – Lord Emsworth's butler for 18 years. Has a mother residing at Eastbourne and helps feed the kidnapped Empress.
(1)	Clarence, Lord Emsworth – 9th Earl and owner of Blandings Castle. A tall, lean man of sixty, he is extremely absent-minded and dotes on the Empress.
(2)	Hugo Carmody – Lord Emsworth's secretary secretly engaged to Millicent
(2)	Lady Constance Keeble – Lord Emsworth's sister living at Blandings
(2)	Millicent Threepwood – Tall, fair daughter of the late Lancelot
(3)	Ronald Overbury Fish – Lord Emsworth's 26 year old nephew who is a member of the Drones Club. An extremely jealous fellow when in love and he's madly in love with Sue.
(3)	Lady Julia Fish – Ronnie's mother, Lord Emsworth's sister and widow of Major General Sir Miles Fish, C.B.O.
(5)	Hon. Galahad Threepwood – Lord Emsworth's short, trim and dapper brother in his late 50's who is writing his reminiscences. Only girl he ever loved was the music-hall singer, Dolly Henderson.
(8)	James – Footman at Blandings
(8)	Thomas – Footman at Blandings
(9)	Empress of Blandings – Lord Emsworth's prize-winning sow. Won the silver medal in the Fat Pigs class at the Shropshire Agricultural Show.
(10)	Sir Gregory Parsloe-Parsloe – Lord Emsworth's 52 year old neighbor. The 7th Baronet lives at Matchingham Hall.
(10)	George Cyril Wellbeloved – Tall, redheaded pigman with a pronounced squint, formerly with Lord Emsworth, now with Sir Gregory
(10)	Pirbright – Lord Emsworth's current pigman

(11)   Rupert J. Baxter — Lord Emsworth's ex-secretary and Connie's helper. Now in the employ of J. Horace Jevons, a Chicago millionaire.

(28)   Sue Brown — Small, orphaned chorus girl in love with Ronnie and a pal to Hugo. Her mother was the famous Dolly Henderson and her father was Jack Cotterleigh of the Irish Guards. Poses as Myra Schoonmaker to gain entry to Blandings.

(31)   Mortimer Mason — Stout senior partner of a theatrical agency and manager of the Regal Theatre. Was fond of Sue's mother and a friend of Gally's.

(40)   Percy Frobisher Pilbeam — Owns the Argus Enquiry Agency. Member of the Junior Constitutional Club who loves Sue.

(74)   Pride of Matchingham — Sir Gregory's pig who is a rival to the Empress. Won second prize at the Shropshire Agricultural Show.

(298)   Voules — Chauffeur at Blandings

Places and Things

(1)   Blandings Castle, Shropshire — Ancestral seat of Lord Emsworth in the village of Market Blandings

(2)   Matchingham Hall, Shropshire — Home of Sir Gregory in the village of Much Matchingham

(31)   Mason and Saxby, Theatrical Enterprises Ltd. — Mortimer Mason is the senior partner

(41)   Junior Constitutional Club — Pilbeam is a member

(74)   Emsworth Arms — Inn at Market Blandings

(91)   Argus Enquiry Agency Ltd. — Pilbeam's detective agency

(98)   Mario's — Restaurant-nightclub in which Pilbeam owns some shares

42a — SUMMER LIGHTNING

First published July 19 1929 by Herbert Jenkins, London, 320 pages. Bound in orange cloth, lettered in black. The edition is identified by "First Printing 1929" on the verso of the title page.

Identical with number 42, save for a dedication to Denis Mackail and a two-page preface.

43 — VERY GOOD, JEEVES

First published June 20 1930 by Doubleday Doran, Garden City, New York, 342 pages. Bound in orange cloth, lettered in black. The first edition is so stated beneath the copyright notice.

The third collection of short stories featuring Bertie Wooster and Jeeves. It contains some of their most famous adventures.

Jeeves and The Impending Doom

Characters

Bertie Wooster

Jeeves

Agatha Gregson — Bertie's mean aunt who wants him to become Filmer's secretary

Rt. Hon. A.B. Filmer — Cabinet Minister staying at Woolam Chersey

Bingo Little — Bertie's childhood friend tutoring Thomas

Thomas Gregson — Aunt Agatha's repulsive son

McIntosh — Aunt Agatha's terrier

Spenser Gregson — Aunt Agatha's husband who is on the Stock Exchange

Purvis — Aunt Agatha's butler

Places

Woollam Chersey — Aunt Agatha's home in Hertfordshire

The Inferiority Complex of Old Sippy

Characters

Bertie Wooster

Jeeves — Doesn't like Bertie's large China vase

(Sippy) Sipperley — Bertie's pal who loves Gwendolen. Editor of the *Mayfair Gazette*.

Gwendolen Moon — Poetess who loves Sippy

Waterbury — Sippy's old headmaster

Places and Things

Mayfair Gazette — Weekly devoted to the lighter interests of society

Novels by Gwendolen — *Autumn Leaves* and *'Twas On An English June*

Jeeves and The Yuletide Spirit

Characters

Bertie Wooster — Once engaged to Honoria but in love with
  Bobbie
Jeeves
Lady Wickham — Aunt Agatha's old friend
Agatha Gregson — Bertie's aunt who wants him to marry
  Honoria
Sir Roderick Glossop — Bertie spikes his hot water bottle
Roberta Wickham — Redheaded girl who is a practical joker
Tuppy Glossop — Sir Roderick's nephew who once played a
  practical joke on Bertie and Bertie tries to get him back

Places and Things

Skeldings Hall — Home of Lady Wickham in Hertfordshire
Drones Club — Bertie and Tuppy are members

Jeeves and The Song of Songs

Characters

Bertie — Attended Oxford with Tuppy and Beefy. Forced to
  sing at Beefy's concert.
Jeeves
Tuppy Glossop — Sings at Beefy's East End entertainment and
  loves Cora
Cora Bellinger — Serious opera singer who performes at Beefy's
  concert
Beefy Bingham — Bertie and Tuppy's school chum who is now a
  parson
Dahlia Travers — Bertie's kind aunt
Angela Travers — Aunt Dahlia's daughter and Bertie's cousin
  who is in love with Tuppy

Places and Things

Jug and Bottle — Pub in the East End
Goat and Grapes — Pub in the East End
**Oddfellows' Hall – Where Beefy's concert took place at
  Bermondsey East**

128

Jeeves and The Dog McIntosh

Characters

Bertie Wooster
Jeeves
McIntosh — Aunt Agatha's terrier
Bobbie Wickham — Wants Blumenfeld to produce her mother's
    play
Blumenfeld — American theatrical producer
Blumenfeld, Jr. — Wants McIntosh

Jeeves and The Spot of Art

Characters

Bertie Wooster — In love with Gwladys
Jeeves
Aunt Dahlia Travers
Anatole
Gwladys Pendlebury — An artist who painted Bertie's portrait
Lucius Pim — An artist who also loves Gwladys
Beatrice Slingsby — Lucius' sister and Alexander's wife
Alexander Slingsby — Jealous owner of Slingsby's Superb
    Soups who uses Bertie's portrait for advertising his soups

Things

Widgeon Seven — Gwladys' red car

Jeeves and The Kid Clementina

Characters

Bertie Wooster
Jeeves — Disapproves of Bertie's bright plus-fours
Miss Mapleton — Aunt Agatha's friend who runs a girls school in
    Bingley
Bobbie Wickham — Gets Bertie involved with Clementina
Clementina — Bobbie's 13 year old cousin who attends St.
    Ethelburga's

Places and Things

Splendide Hotel — Where Bertie stayed at Bingley-on-Sea for
    the Drones Club golf tournament

129

St. Ethelburga's — Miss Mapleton's girls school

Jeeves and The Love That Purifies

Characters

Bertie Wooster
Jeeves
(Sippy) Oliver Randolph Sipperley
Gwendolen Moon — Engaged to Sippy
Sebastian Moon — Gwendolen's young brother
Dahlia Travers — Makes a bet with Jane pitting Anatole against
    Jane's kitchen maid
Bonzo — Dahlia's young son
Anstruther — Dahlia's father's old friend
Thomas — Aunt Agatha's 13 year old son
Jack, Lord Snettisham
Jane Snettisham — Jack's wife and Aunt Dahlia's friend

Places

Brinkley Court — Aunt Dahlia's home in Worcestershire

Jeeves and The Old School Chum

Characters

Bertie Wooster
Jeeves
(Bingo) Richard Little
George — Bertie's uncle
Rosie Little — Bingo's wife
Laura Pyke — Rosie's schoolmate who is a food crank

Things

Novels by Rosie M. Banks (Little) — *Mervyn Keene, Clubman*
    and *Only A Factory Girl*

The Indian Summer of An Uncle

Characters

Bertie Wooster
Jeeves

George, Lord Yaxley — Bertie's extremely fat uncle who thinks he loves Rhoda. Winds up engaged to the only girl he ever really loved, Maudie.

Rhoda Platt — Waitress at the Buffers

Agatha Gregson — Bertie's aunt

Maud Wilberforce — Ex-barmaid at the Criterion. Loved George years ago but his family bought her off.

Places and Things

Drones Club — Bertie is a member

Buffers Club — Uncle George is a member

Wisteria Lodge — Rhoda's house in Kitchener Road, East Dulwich

Tuppy Changes His Mind

Characters

Bertie Wooster

Jeeves

Sir Reginald Witherspoon, Bart. — Married to Uncle Tom's younger sister, Katherine

Tuppy Glossop — Sort of engaged to Angela but infatuated with Miss Dalgleish

Dahlia Travers

Angela Travers — Dahlia's daughter who loves Tuppy

Miss Dalgleish — Loves dogs

Mulready — Sir Reginald's butler

Places and Things

Bleaching Court — Sir Reginald's house in Upper Bleaching, Hampshire

Drones Club

Hockley-cum-Meston — Rival village

Green Pig — Pub in Hockley

43a – VERY GOOD, JEEVES

First published July 4 1930 by Herbert Jenkins, London, 320 pages. Bound in orange cloth, lettered in black. "First Printing 1930" on the verso of the title page.

Contains a dedication to E. Phillips Oppenheim and a preface not in number 43. Except for the following, the text is identical:

Jeeves and The Spot of Art

The Spot of Art

Jeeves and The Kid Clementina

St. Ethelburga's becomes St. Monica's

Tuppy Changes His Mind

Title becomes **The Ordeal of Young Tuppy**

44 — BIG MONEY

First published January 30 1931 by Doubleday Doran, Garden City, New York 316 pages. Bound in orange cloth, title on dark green background lettered in orange. The first edition is so stated beneath the copyright notice.

Utilizes Valley Fields as the background. The following passages are especially recommended: The Man With the Beard (pp 64-65), The Beard and the Barmaid (pp 88-91), Stolen Hats and Broken Windows (pp 117-130), The Bassinger Ball (pp 141-155), and Working Up To A Proposal (pp 243-256).

Characters

(1)   (Biscuit) Godfrey Edward Winstanley Brent, Lord Biskerton — Berry's redheaded school chum with a slight moustache. Engaged to Ann but loves Kitchie.

(1)   (Berry) John Beresford Conway — 25 year old hero who inherited a supposedly worthless copper mine. Loves Ann and poses as a secret service agent.

(3)   Torquil Paterson Frisby — Small, American millionaire with dyspepsia who falls in love with Vera

(4)   Hannah Wisdom — Berry's old nurse and housekeeper

(6)   Ebenezer Attwater — Berry's later aunt's lawyer who lends him money

(8)   Lady Vera Mace — The Biscuit's aunt, the Earl's sister, and widow of Colonel Archibald Mace, C.V.O., who has a compelling personality

(8)   **George, Lord Hoddesdon** — 6th Earl and father of the Biscuit

(15)   Josephine Moon — Frisby's sister

(16)   Ann Margaret Moon — Frisby's niece who wants a Sir Galahad type. Heroine engaged to the Biscuit but loves Berry.

(34)   J. Bernard Hoke — Frisby's stooge who double-crosses him. Tries to swindle Berry out of the Dream Come True.

(37)   Captain Kelly — Hoke's shady partner

(45)   Major Everard Flood-Smith — Berry's neighbor

(47)   (Kitchie) Katherine Valentine — Small, blonde American niece of the Major's who is loved by the Biscuit

(98)   Mr. Cornelius — Valley Fields house agent with a long white beard

(105)   Merwyn Flock — American actor to whom Kitchie is engaged

(109)	Venner — The Biscuit's manservant
(112)	Sham-Poo — Lady Vera's Pekingese
(133)	Sergeant Finbow — Policeman in Valley Fields who is engaged to Hannah
(161)	Mr. Robbins — Frisby's lawyer
(167)	Mr. Bellamy — Hoke's lawyer
(271)	Oofy Simpson — Wealthiest member of the Drones Club

Places and Things

(1)	Drones Club — Lord Biskerton is a member
(2)	Valley Fields — Suburb of London where Berry lives
(13)	Dream Come True — Berry owns controlling stock of apparent dud mine
(14)	6, Pudding Lane, E.C. 4 — Frisby's office address
(30)	Horned Toad, Inc. — Frisby heads the syndicate of this copper mine
(41)	Edgeling Court, Sussex — Home of the Hoddesdon family
(44)	The Nook, Mulberry Grove — Berry's semi-detached home in Valley Fields
(45)	Castlewood — House owned by Major Flood-Smith in Valley Fields
(45)	Peacehaven — Biscuit's house next to Berry's
(56)	Hawes and Dawes — Outfitters of shirts, ties and linens
(56)	Dykes, Dykes and Pinweed — Bespoke Tailors and Breeches makers
(79)	Galliwell and Gooch — Sells shoes and bootings
(80)	Jolly Harvesters — Pub in Esher
(98)	Matters and Cornelius — House agents at Valley Fields
(163)	Robbins, Robbins, Robbins, and Robbins — Soliciters
(204)	Mario's — Restaurant and nightclub

44a — BIG MONEY

First published March 20 1931 by Herbert Jenkins, London, 320 pages. Bound in orange cloth, lettered in black. "First Printing 1931" on the verso of the title page. Identical with number 44.

45 – IF I WERE YOU

First published September 3 1931 by Doubleday Doran, Garden City, New York, 306 pages. Bound in orange cloth, lettered in dark brown. The first edition is so stated beneath the copyright notice.

An easily read story whose gags are slightly forced. The plot was taken from Anstey's *Vice Versa*. Dramatized as *Who's Who* in collaboration with Guy Bolton, to whom this edition is dedicated.

Characters

(1)   Anthony Claude Wilbraham Bryce, Chalk-Marshall, 5th Earl of Bryce Chalk-Marshall, 5th Earl of Droitwich – 30 year old hero engaged to Violet but loves Polly

(1)   Charles – Lord Droitwich's footman

(2)   Theodore Slingsby – Lord Droitwich's butler and Syd's uncle

(3)   Lady Lydia Bassinger – Lord Droitwich's aunt in her mid-forties

(4)   Hon. Frederick Chalk-Marshall – Tony's younger brother

(7)   Sir Herbert Bassinger – Lydia's husband

(8)   Violet Waddington – Tall, slender and beautiful heiress engaged to Tony

(8)   Tubby, Lord Bridgnorth – Freddie's friend and gossip writer

(11)   G.G. Waddington – Violet's father, a millionaire of the 97 Soups

(15)   (Ma) Bella Price – Tony's nurse and Slingsby's sister

(15)   Sydney Lancelot Price – A Socialist barber in Knightsbridge who thinks he's the real Lord Droitwich

(43)   Polly Brown – Heroine American manicurist at Syd's shop with brains. Loves Tony.

(121)   George Christopher Meech – Barber in Syd's shop

(130)   Luella Beamish – Tubby's American Fiancee

(254)   J.G. Weatherby – Lawyer for Lord Droitwich

Places and Things

(1)   Langley End, Worcestershire – Country seat of Lord Droitwich

(20)   Droitwich Arms -- Village pub

(120)   Price's Hygienic Toilet Saloon – Syd's barber shop in Mott Street, Knightsbridge

(131)   Drones Club – Freddie and Tubby are members

(135)   Caterpiller and Jug – Pub in Knightsbridge near Syd's shop

135

(154) Price's Derma Vitalis — Syd's grandfather invented this prepara-
       tion for the growth of hair
(260) Polk, Weatherby, Polk & Polk — Law firm

45a – IF I WERE YOU

First published September 25 1931 by Herbert Jenkins, London,
288 pages. Bound in orange cloth, lettered in black. "First Printing
1931" on the verso of the title page. Identical with number 45, though
lacking the dedication.

First published March 10 1932 by Faber and Faber, London, 288 pages. Bound in yellow cloth, lettered in green. "First published in mcmxxxii" on the verso of the title page. The only Wodehouse title to be published by Faber, it is also Wodehouse's only book of humorous articles. Sheets of this first edition have also been bound in other colors, but are of later issue.

These articles were originally written for the American magazine, *Vanity Fair,* during the later teens. They have been tidied up here. In subsequent volumes *(America, I Like You, Over Seventy,* and *Author! Author!)* some of these and other articles have been reprinted, with additional bits of autobiography.

The Hollywood Scandal

To The Editor – Sir. . .

My Gentle Readers

Thrillers

Fair Play for Audiences

Looking Back At The Halls

An Outline of Shakespeare

The Decay of Falconry

A Day With The Swattesmore

Prospects For Wambledon

Fashionable Weddings and Smart Divorces

Happy Christmas and Merry New Year

Thoughts On The Income Tax

Butlers and The Buttled

A Word About Amusement Parks

Roulette

Chemin De Fer

On Ocean Liners

Photographs and Photographers

138

47 – DOCTOR SALLY

First published April 7 1932 by Methuen & Co., London, 156 pages. Bound in blue cloth, lettered in black. "First Published in 1932" on the verso of the title page.

A short novel taken from Wodehouse's play, *Good Morning, Bill.* Published in the United States under the title "The Medicine Girl" in the short story collection, number 57a. The ending is a drawn-out version of a similar scene sketched out in number 40.

Characters

(1)   Sir Hugo Drake — Eminent nerve specialist. Bill's uncle and a golf addict.
(2)   Dr. Sally Smith — Small, pretty general practitioner. American who loves golf and likes those who work.
(3)   William Bannister — Drake's nephew who owns a stock and dairy farm in Hampshire. Falls in love with Sally.
(8)   Marie — Mrs. Higginbotham's maid
(9)   Lottie Higginbotham — Widow of a millionaire. Formerly married to Squiffy.
(10)   (Squiffy Bixby) Lord Tidmouth — Old school chum of Bill's

Places and Things

(1)   Bingley-on-Sea — Resort on the south coast of England. A haven for golfers.
(8)   Hotel Superba — At Bingley-on-Sea
(13)   The Manor, Woollam Chersey — Bill's home in Hampshire
(21-22) " 'Ever spoken to her?'
         'No, I haven't the nerve. She's so far above me.'
         'Tall girl, eh?'
         'Spiritually, you ass!' "
(97)   " 'Well, naturally,' he said with dignity, halting once more, 'I have had — er — experiences — like other men.'
         Sally was at the stethoscope again.
         'Um-hum,' she said.
         'I admit it. There *have* been women in my life.'
         'Say ninety-nine.'
         'Not half as many as that!' cried Bill, starting.
         'Say ninety-nine, please.'
         'Oh!' Bill became calmer. 'I didn't — I thought — I imagined that you were referring — Well, in short, ninety-nine.' "

139

First published August 17 1932 by both Herbert Jenkins, London, 320 pages, and Doubleday Doran, Garden City, New York, 308 pages. Jenkins edition bound in orange cloth, lettered in black, with "First Printing 1932" on the verso of the title page. Doubleday edition bound in black pictorial cloth, lettered in orange, with six illustrations by Rea Irvin. The illustration on page 99 is repeated on the title page and front cover. First edition so stated beneath the copyright notice. Both editions dedicated to Maureen O'Sullivan. Editions identical to one another. Wodehouse, collaborating with Guy Bolton, turned the novel into their play, *The Inside Stand.*

Page numbering here follows the Jenkins edition. An hilarious moment is when the Two French Scholars meet (pp 160-169).

Characters

(9)   J. Wellington Gedge — Short, fat, American from California, dominated by his wife

(10)   Medway — Mrs. Gedge's maid who is a crook known as Gun-Shoe Gertie, wanting to steal the Gedge jewelery. Used to work with Oily.

(10)   Julia Gedge — Widow of millionaire oilman Wilmot Brewster who wants her husband to be the U.S. Ambassador to France. Soup's ex-partner in crime.

(10)   Kate Amelia Putnam — Julia's social secretary and detective from the James B. Flaherty Agency

(13)   Senator Ambrose Opal — Fat American senator who sponsors legislation against drink, but he mops the stuff up. Wants Jane to marry Packy.

(13)   Jane Opal — The Senator's black-haired and pretty daughter who is secretly engaged to Blair, but loves Packy

(13)   (Veek) Vicomte Maurice de Blissac — Packy's friend

(18)   (Oily) Gordon Carlisle — American con man in St. Rocque posing as the Duc de Pont-Andemer

(18)   Soup Slattery — American safe-cracker who is afraid of Pekes

(35)   (Packy) Patrick B. Franklyn — American millionaire who went to Yale and played football. Engaged to Lady Beatrice but loves Jane.

(35)   Lady Beatrice Bracken — Daughter of the Earl of Stableford engaged to Packy

140

(37)   Blair Eggleston — Young novelist who is engaged to Jane. Works as a Sound Effects man for the BBC and becomes Senator Opal's valet
(206)   Octave — Local policeman engaged to the Chateau's cook

Places and Things

(9)   Chateau Blissac — The Gedge's rented home in St. Rocque, Brittany
(17)   Hotel des Etrangers — Best hotel in St. Rocque
(35)   Worbles — Earl of Stableford's home in Dorsetshire
(37)   *Worm i' the Root* — Blair's novel
(236)   *Offal* — Blair's novel

141

49 – MULLINER NIGHTS

First published January 17 1933 by Herbert Jenkins, London, 320 pages. Bound in orange cloth, lettered in black. "First Printing 1933" on the verso of the title page.

The third and last volume of stories dealing exclusively with Mr. Mulliner. Wodehouse is in top form throughout, "The Smile That Wins" and "Strychnine in the Soup" finding especial favor with anthologists.

The Smile That Wins

Characters

Mr. Mulliner

Miss Postlethwaite

Pint of Stout, Whisky Sour and Mild and Bitter — Mr. Mulliner's companions

Adrian Mulliner — Dark, thin and melancholy nephew. A detective with dyspepsia and a curious smile, he loves Millicent.

Lady Millicent Shipton-Bellinger — Loves Adrian

Reginald Alexander Montacute James Bramfylde Tregennis Shipton-Bellinger, the 5th Earl of Brangbolton — Lady Millicent's father who wants her to marry Sir Jasper. Plays Persian Monarchs.

Sir Jasper Addleton, O.B.E. — Bald and fat financier in love with Millicent

Sir Sutton Hartley-Wesping, Bart. — Invites Adrian to his country house

The Very Reverend the Dean of Bittlesham — Performed at the wedding of Adrian and Millicent

Places and Things

Widgery and Boon — Adrian's firm of investigators of Albermarle Street

Senior Bloodstain — Club for detectives in Rupert Street and of which Adrian is a member

Wesping Hall — Sir Sutton's home at Wesping Parva, Sussex

The Story of Webster

Characters

Mr. Mulliner

Pint of Bitter, Lemon Sour and Small Bass — Mr. Mulliner's
    companions

Lancelot Mulliner — Cousin Edward's son, a 25 year old artist

Theodore Bongo-Bongo, Dean of Bolsover — Lancelot's rich
    uncle who became a Bishop

Gladys Bingley — Engaged to Lancelot, known as The Sweet
    Singer of Garbidge Mews, Fulham

Webster — Uncle Theodore's cat

Brenda Carberry-Pirbright — Lancelot's fiancee, a pill whose
    portrait he painted

Bernard Worple — Lancelot's friend who is a neo-vorticist
    sculpter

Rodney Scollop — Lancelot's friend who is a surrealist painter

Cats Will Be Cats

Characters

Mr. Mulliner

Whisky and Splash, Small Port, Pint of Bitter, Lemon Sour and
    Rum and Milk — Mr. Mulliner's companions

Lancelot Mulliner — Artist engaged to Gladys

Webster — Lancelot's uncle's cat

Gladys Bingley — Engaged to Lancelot

Theodore, Bishop of Bongo-Bongo — Lancelot's wealthy uncle
    who loves his cat

Lady Widdrington — Sir George's widow who loves Theodore
    and cats, but not Webster

Mrs. Pulteney-Banks — Lady Widdrington's mother

Percy — Lady Widdrington's mean cat

Fotheringay — Lady Widdrington's butler

Places

Widdrington Manor — Lady Widdrington's home in Bottleby-in-
    the-Vale, Hampshire

143

The Knightly Quest of Mervyn

Characters

Mr. Mulliner

Stout and Mild, Ninepennyworth of Sherry, Rum and Milk — Mr. Mulliner's companions

Mervyn Mulliner — Cousin's son. A chump in love with Clarice.

Clarice Mallaby — Asks Mervyn to get her some strawberries in December

(Oofy) Alexander G. Prosser — Mervyn's rich young friend who also admires Clarice

Joseph, The Earl of Blotsam — Mervyn's maternal uncle

Places and Things

Restless Cheese — Nightclub

Bellamy's — Bespoke fruitists in Piccadilly where strawberries can be purchased

Blotsam Castle — The Earl's home in Blotsam Regis, Shropshire

Blotto Kitten — Nightclub.

The Voice From The Past

Characters

Mr. Mulliner

Tankard of Stout — Mr. Mulliner's companion

Sacheverell Mulliner — Nephew who went to Harborough

The Rev. J.G. Smethurst — Headmaster at Harborough College, now the Bishop of Bognor

Muriel Branksome — Hearty, breezy girl engaged to Sacheverell, formerly engaged to Bernard

Lt. Col. Sir Redvers Branksome — Muriel's tough, horsey father

Jno. B. Philbrick — Manager of the correspondence school

Bernard — Muriel's cousin in the Guards

Places and Things

Leave-It-To-Us Correspondence School — Supposed to send Sacheverell a course in Scientific Agriculture but sends him one on how to gain confidence

Branksome Towers — Sir Redvers' home at Market Branksome

Scalpo — "It Fertilizes the Follicles"

Soothine — After shave lotion

Doctor Wilberforce's Golden Gargle — patent medicine

Open House

Characters

Mr. Mulliner

Eustace Mulliner — 24 year old nephew in the Swiss embassy in love with Marcella

Marcella Tyrrwhitt — Loved by Eustace

William — Marcella's canary

Reginald — Marcella's Peke

Beatrice Watterson — Eustace's former flame who took Reginald

Blenkinsop – Eustace's valet

Orlando Wotherspoon — Eustace's large and unpleasant neighbor who is the vice president of Our Dumb Chums' League

Francis — Aunt Georgiana's cat

Georgiana, Lady Beazley-Beazley – Eustace's rich widowed aunt

Place

Wittleford-cum-Bagsley-on-Sea — Where Aunt Georgiana lives

Best Seller

Characters

Mr. Mulliner

Miss Postlethwaite

Stout and Bitter — Mr. Mulliner's companion

Egbert Mulliner — Nephew who loves and marries Evangeline. Assistant editor of *The Weekly Booklover.*

Evangeline Pembury — Loves Egbert and writes a novel

Jno. Henderson Banks — Evangeline's handsome literary agent

Places and Things

Parted Ways and *Rue for Remembrance* — Evangeline's novels

The Weekly Booklover — Magazine for which Egbert is Assistant Editor

Burwash Bay — Resort area

Mainprice and Peabody — Evangeline's publishers

Strychnine In The Soup

Characters

Mr. Mulliner

Draught Stout, Lemonade and Angostura, Small Lager — Mr. Mulliner's companions

Cyril Mulliner — Nephew, an interior decorator who loves mystery stories and Amelia

Amelia Bassett — Loves Cyril and mystery stories

Lady Bassett — Amelia's mother who also loves mysteries, a big-game hunter and explorer

Lester Mapledurham (pronounced Mum) — Explorer and big-game hunter

Places and Things

The Grey Vampire — Mystery play

Blood on the Banisters, Severed Throats, Gore by the Gallon and *The Missing Toe* — Mystery novels

Strychnine in the Soup — Mystery novel by Horatio Slingsby

Barkley Towers — Sir Mortimer and Lady Wingham's home at Barkley Regis

Gala Night

Characters

Mr. Mulliner

Stout and Mild, Sherry and Bitters, Whiskey Sour, Lemonade and Angostura — Mr. Mulliner's companions

The Rev. Augustine Mulliner — Nephew who is now a Vicar

Ronald Bracy-Gascoigne — Engaged to Hypatia and loves dancing

Jane Mulliner — Augustine's wife who is ill

Hypatia Wace — Jane's school friend. Niece and ward of the Bishop of Stortford

Percy, Bishop of Stortford — Augustine's superior

Pricilla — The Bishop's wife

Places and Things

Mulliner's Buck-U-Uppo — Tonic invented by Mr. Mulliner's brother, Wilfred

146

Walsingford-below-Chiveney-on-Thames — Augustine is Vicar in
    the resort area
Home From Home — Nightclub

49a — MULLINER NIGHTS

First published February 15 1933 by Doubleday Doran, Garden
City, New York, 312 pages. Bound in orange pictorial cloth, lettered in
black. First edition so stated beneath the copyright notice. Identical
with number 49.

First published July 28 1933 by Little, Brown and Co., Boston, 316 pages. Bound in black pictorial cloth, lettered in red. "Published July, 1933" beneath the copyright notice.

The fourth in the Blandings series is a direct sequel to number 42.

Characters

(3)	George Alexander Pyke, Lord Tilbury — Short, fat owner of the Mammoth Publishing Company who wants to publish Gally's reminiscences. He loves pigs and has a farm in Buckinghamshire.
(3)	Lady Julia Fish — Large, blonde and commanding sister of Lord Emsworth and Gally
(4)	(Gally) Hon. Galahad Threepwood — Lord Emsworth's 57 year old brother who wrote his reminiscences
(6)	Sir Gregory Parsloe-Parsloe — 7th Baronet and Lord Emsworth's neighbor. Monty's uncle.
(8)	Ronald Overbury Fish — Lady Julia's son engaged to Sue
(9)	(Monty) Montague Bodkin — Sir Gregory's nephew and Assistant editor of *Tiny Tots*. Member of the Drones Club who becomes Lord Emsworth's new secretary. Formerly engaged to Sue, now engaged to Gertrude Butterwick.
(13)	The Rev. Aubrey Sellick — Editor of *Tiny Tots*
(21)	Hugo Carmody — Lord Emsworth's secretary for eleven weeks
(22)	Clarence, Lord Emsworth — Tall, thin and scraggly 60 year old 9th Earl who loves the Empress. Ronnie's trustee.
(23)	Empress of Blandings — Lord Emsworth's prize pig
(23)	Beach — Butler at Blandings for 18 years. Asked to hide Galahad's manuscript.
(25)	Pride of Matchingham — Sir Gregory's pig, rival of the Empress's
(27)	Sue Brown — Ronnie's 19 year old fiancee
(30)	Lady Constance Keeble — Lord Emsworth's dominating sister
(31)	Percy Frobisher Pilbeam — Runs the Argus Private Inquiry Agency
(36)	Voules — Chauffeur at Blandings
(37)	Jas. Pirbright — Lord Emsworth's pigman
(45)	George Cyril Wellbeloved — Lord Emsworth's former pigman now in the employ of Sir Gregory

(64)   J.G. Butterwick — Gertrude's father who is the head of Butterwick, Price & Mandelbaum, exporters and importers
(78)   Robinson — Cab driver at Market Blandings
(125) Buckingham Big Boy — Lord Tilbury's pig
(145) Fosberry — Vicar at Market Blandings
(246) Angus McAllister — Lord Emsworth's Scottish head gardener
(281) Webber — Veterinarian at Market Blandings
(299) Stokes — First footman at Blandings
(299) Thomas — Second footman at Blandings

Places and Things

(3)   Mammoth Publishing Company — Owned by Lord Tilbury on Fleet St.
(3)   Tilbury House — Building which houses the Mammoth Publishing Co.
(4)   *Tiny Tots* — Mammoth's magazine for children
(4)   Blandings Castle — Lord Emsworth's home in Shropshire
(6)   Matchingham Hall — Sir Gregory's home
(6)   *Society Spice* — Mammoth's magazine for gossips
(15)   Drones Club — Monty Bodkin is a member
(20)   Bunch of Grapes — Pub in Fleet St.
(29)   Market Blandings — Nearest village to the Castle
(51)   Pelican Club — Gally was a member of the now defunct club
(114) Emsworth Arms — Inn at Market Blandings serving the best beer
(148) Pubs at Market Blandings — The Wheatsheaf, The Waggoner's Rest, The Beetle and Wedge, The Stitch in Time, and The Jolly Cricketeers
(176) Riggs' Golden Balm — Embrocation

50a — HEAVY WEATHER

First published August 10 1933 by Herbert Jenkins, London, 320 pages. Bound in blue cloth, lettered in orange. "First Printing 1933" on the verso of the title page. Identical with number 50.

51 – THANK YOU, JEEVES

First published March 16 1934 by Herbert Jenkins, London, 320 pages. Bound in stone-colored cloth, lettered in red. "First Printed 1934" on the verso of the title page.
The first of the Jeeves novels.

Characters

(7) Bertie Wooster — Went to Eton and Oxford with Chuffy and had an Uncle Henry who loved pigs. Dissention with Jeeves over Bertie's playing the Banjolele.

(7) Jeeves — Leaves Bertie's employ to work for Chuffy. Leaves Chuffy to go temporarily to Stoker's and then back to Bertie.

(7) J. Washburn Stoker — American millionaire who inherited fifty million dollars from his cousin George. Talked into buying Chuffnell Hall for Glossop.

(7) Pauline Stoker — Bertie's ex-fiancee, Stoker's daughter who is in love with Chuffy. Dynamic girl.

(8) Sir Roderick Glossop — Nerve specialist who is engaged to Aunt Myrtle

(8) (Chuffy) Marmaduke, Lord Chuffnell — Bertie's school chum and 5th Baron

(13) Ben Bloom — Leader at the Alhambra of his Sixteen Baltimore Buddies

(15) Mrs. Tinkler-Moulke — A patient of Glossop's who owns a Pomeranian and lives in a flat beneath Bertie's

(22) Myrtle, Lady Chuffnell – Chuffy's aunt and Seabury's mother who loves Glossop

(22) Seabury — Aunt Myrtle's 12 year old son

(25) Ted Voules — Police-Sergeant at Chuffnell Regis who plays the harmonium

(31) Brinkley — Bertie's new valet at Chuffnell Regis who is a Bolshevik

(41) Dwight Stoker — Washburn's young son

(60) Benstead — Jeeves' friend who was valet to the late multimillionaire, George Stoker

(107) Constable Dobson — Voules' nephew and policeman at Chuffnell Regis

(17)   Berkeley Mansions — Bertie's flat in London
(22)   Chuffnell Hall — Chuffy's estate in Chuffnell Regis, Somerset-
            shire·
(22)   Dower House — Aunt Myrtle's home on the estate
(23)   Drones Club — Bertie, Freddie Oaker and Catsmeat Potter-
            Pirbright are members
(29)   Seaview Cottage — Cottage on Chuffy's estate which Bertie
            rents and burns down
(115)   Widgeon Seven — Bertie's two-seater
(224)   Chuffnell Arms — Pub in village

51a — THANK YOU, JEEVES

First published April 23 1934 by Little, Brown and Co., Boston,
308 pages. Bound in plum pictorial cloth, lettered in black. "Published
April, 1934" on the verso of the title page. Identical with number 51.

52 – RIGHT HO, JEEVES

First published October 5 1934 by Herbert Jenkins, London, 320 pages. Bound in off-white cloth, lettered in red. "MCMXXXIV" appears on the bottom of the title page, but the title lacks the customary "First Printing" notice on the verso of the title page.

The second novel to feature Bertie and Jeeves, containing one of the most memorable drunk scenes in all English literature when Gussie Presents the Prizes (pp 190-231). Another hilarious highspot involves linguistics in the Doings in Anatole's Bedroom (pp 247-259). A Wodehouse classic.

Characters

(9)   Bertie Wooster — Gussie's school chum

(9)   Jeeves — Formerly in the employ of the late Lord Brancaster. Disapproves of Bertie's white mess jacket.

(10)   Dahlia Travers — Bertie's kind, bluff and hearty aunt who married Tom Travers. Has daughter Angela and runs the weekly woman's magazine, *Milady's Boudoir.*

(10)   Angela Travers — Bertie's cousin engaged, more or less, to Tuppy

(10)   (Tuppy) Hildebrand Glossop — Honoria's cousin who loves food. Engaged to Angela and who once bet Bertie that he couldn't swing across the swimming bath at the Drones by the rings. As Bertie attempted this feat, Tuppy brought the last ring back, forcing Bertie to drop into the bath with his clothes on.

(10)   Tom Travers — Dahlia's millionaire husband

(11)   (Gussie) Augustus Fink-Nottle — Shy school chum of Bertie's who lives in a small village in Lincolnshire where he studies Newts. Loves and finally gets engaged to Madeline.

(18)   Madeline Bassett — Blonde, dreamy girl with a strong profile who loves Gussie but, in a fit of pique, gets engaged to Bertie. Finally she gets together with Gussie.

(44)   Anatole — Aunt Dahlia's incomparable French chef

(132)   Seppings — Butler at Brinkley Court

(287)   Waterbury — Chauffeur at Brinkley Court

Places and Things

(11)   Brinkley Court — Dahlia and Tom's estate near Market Snods-
        bury, Worcestershire
(11)   Drones·Club — Bertie, Tuppy, Freddie Widgeon and Pongo
        Twistleton are members
(39)   *Milady's Boudoir* — Woman's weekly magazine owned by Aunt
        Dahlia

52a — BRINKLEY MANOR

First published October 15 1934 by Little, Brown & Co., Boston,
324 pages. Bound in red pictorial cloth, lettered in black. "Published
October, 1934" beneath the copyright notice.

Brinkley Court becomes Brinkley Manor. Otherwise identical with
number 52.

First published April 12 1935 by Herbert Jenkins, London, 320 pages. Bound in light green cloth, lettered in black. "First printing 1935" on the verso of the title page.

The subtitle, "And Elsewhere" indicates that not all the short stories are about the Blandings inhabitants. The first six however are, and Wodehouse in a preface indicates that in point of time they properly come after *Leave it to Psmith* (number 32) and before *Fish Preferred* (number 42). It is in "Pig-Hoo-o-o-o-ey" that the Empress wins her first medal as champion in the Fat Pigs Class at the annual Shropshire Agricultural Show. "Lord Emsworth and the Girl Friend" is an outstanding short story in all respects.

The Custody of The Pumpkin

Characters

Angus McAllister — Lord Emsworth's head gardener
Hon. Freddie Threepwood — Lord Emsworth's 26 year old second son who gets engaged and then marries Aggie
Lord Emsworth — Fluffy-minded, amiable peer who wins first prize for his pumpkin. This pumpkin phase preceded the more lasting sow adoration.
Beach — Butler at Blandings
(Aggie) Niagara Donaldson — Rich American girl who marries Freddie
Sir Gregory Parsloe-Parsloe — Lord Emsowrth's rival in the pumpkin contest
Blandings Hope — Lord Emsworth's pumpkin
Robert Barker — Lord Emsworth's second gardener
Mr. Donaldson — American millionaire whose daughter married Freddie

Places and Things

Blandings Castle — Lord Emsworth's home
Matchingham Hall — Sir Gregory's home
Senior Conservative Club — Lord Emsworth is a member
Donaldson's Dog-Biscuits — Firm owned by Mr. Donaldson

Lord Emsworth Acts For The Best

Characters

Beach — Butler at Blandings
Mrs. Twemlow — Housekeeper at Blandings
Lord Emsworth
Hon. Frederick Threepwood
Aggie — Freddie's wife
Jane Yorke — Aggie's friend who wants her to marry Jane's
  brother

Pig-Hoo-o-o-o-ey!

Characters

Clarence, Lord Emsworth — Loves the Empress
Empress of Blandings — Won first prize in the Fat Pigs Class at
  the 87th Annual Shropshire Agricultural Show
George Cyril Wellbeloved — Lord Emsworth's 29 year old
  pigman
Evans — Police Constable in Market Blandings
Lady Constance Keeble
Dr. Smithers — Veterinary Surgeon in Market Blandings
Lord Heacham — Rich landowner whose engagement to Angela
  is broken
Angela — Lord Emsworth's 21 year old niece who breaks her
  engagement to Lord Heacham because she wants to marry
  James
James Bartholomew Belford — Worked on a farm in Nebraska.
  Loves Angela and teaches Lord Emsworth the master pig call.
Beach

Places and Things

The Bridgnorth, Shifnal, and Albrighton Argus (with which is
  incorporated *The Wheat Growers' Intelligencer and Stock
  Breeders' Gazetteer*) — Local newspaper
Goat and Feather — Pub in Market Blandings
Senior Conservative Club — Lord Emsworth is a member

Company For Gertrude

Characters

Hon. Freddie Threepwood — Tries to sell his aunt, Georgiana, Donaldson's Dog Joy

Georgiana, Lady Alcester – Freddie's aunt who owns many dogs One of the many sisters of Lord Emsworth.

(Beefy) The Rev. Rupert Bingham — Freddie's pal from his University days who wants to marry Gertrude

Gertrude — Georgiana's beautiful 23 year old daughter in love with Beefy

Clarence, Lord Emsworth — 59 year old peer who likes to try new medicines. Likes to potter in his gardens. His father lived to be 77.

Sir Gregory Parsloe-Parsloe — Stole Lord Emsworth's pigman away

George Cyril Wellbeloved — Lord Emsworth's ex-pigman, now with Sir Gregory

Beach — Butler at Blandings

Places and Things

Donaldson's Dog Joy — Dog biscuits manufactured by Freddie's father-in-law

Blandings Castle

Matchingham Hall — Sir Gregory's home in Much Matchingham

The Go-Getter

Characters

Hon. Freddie Threepwood — Tries to promote Donaldson's Dog Joy

Georgiana, Lady Alcester — Freddie's aunt who has 14 dogs

Gertrude — Engaged to Beefy but infatuated with Orlo

Beefy Bingham — Vicar at Much Matchingham engaged to Gertrude

Orlo Watkins — A crooning tenor

Bottles — Beefy's dog

Lady Constance Keeble

Beach

Places and Things

Blandings Castle
Emsworth Arms
Blue Boar — Pub in Much Matchingham
Cow and Caterpiller — Pub on the Shrewsbury Road

Lord Emsworth and The Girl Friend

Characters

Clarence, 9th Earl of Emsworth
Lady Constance Keeble
Angus McAllister — Lord Emsworth's head gardener for nine
   years, who wants a gravel path put through the yew alley
Gladys — 12 or 13 year old London girl who likes Lord
   Emsworth
Ern — Gladys' small brother

Places and Things

Blandings Castle
Blandings Parva — Nearest hamlet to the Castle

Mr. Potter Takes A Rest Cure

Characters

John Hamilton Potter — Founder and proprietor of J.H. Potter,
   Inc., a New York publishing house
Clifford Gandle — An obnoxious M.P. who proposes to Bobbie
Lady Wickham — Bobbie's mother who wants her to marry
   Gandle
(Bobbie) Roberta Wickham — Slim and boyish redhead who
   loves playing pranks
(Algy) Algernon Crufts — Bobbie's friend

Places and Things

Skeldings Hall — Lady Wickham's home
Pen and Ink Club — Lady Wickham is a member
Prodder and Wiggs — Publishers of Gandle's political book
Watchman, What of The Night? — Gandle's book

Monkey Business

Characters

Mr. Mulliner

A Tankard of Stout, Small Bass, Gin Fizz — Mr. Mulliner's companions

Miss Postlethwaite

Montrose Mulliner — Timid distant cousin who is Assistant Director of the Perfecto-Zizzbaum Motion Picture Corp. of Hollywood

Rosalie Beamish — Engaged to Montrose

Mr. Schnellenhamer — President of Perfecto-Zizzbaum

George Pybus — Montrose's friend who works in the Press Department

Cyril Waddesley-Davenport — Actor who attended Oxford who plays the part of a gorilla

The Nodder

Characters

Mr. Mulliner

Rum and Milk, Whiskey and Splash, A Pint of Half-and-Half — Mr. Mulliner's companions

Wilmot Mulliner — Distant cousin, a nodder who loves Mabel

Mabel Potter — Mr. Schnellenhamer's private secretary, an ex-bird imitator in Vaudeville

Mr. Schnellenhamer — President of the movie company

Little Johnny Bingley — Child movie star who is in reality a middle-aged midget

Things

Perfecto-Zizzbaum Corp. — Movie company in Hollywood

The Juice of An Orange

Characters

Mr. Mulliner

Ernest Biggs — Landlord of the Angler's Rest

Wilmot Mulliner — Distant cousin

Mabel Potter — Breaks off her engagement to Wilmot

Eustiss Vanderleigh — Playwright
Mr. Schnellenhamer
Mr. Levitsky
Hortensia Burwash — The Empress of Molten Passion at P.Z.

The Rise of Minna Nordstrom

Characters

Mr. Mulliner
Miss Postlethwaite
Rum and Milk, Sherry and Bitters, Port from the Wood, Dry
    Martini — Mr. Mulliner's companions
Jacob Z. Schnellenhamer
Vera Prebble — Mr. Schnellenhamer's pretty parlour-maid who
    turns into Minna
Isidore Fishbein — Head of Perfecto-Fishbein
Ben Zizzbaum — Head of Zizzbaum-Celluloid Corp.
Sigismund Glutz — Head of Medulla-Oblongata-Glutz

Things

Perfecto-Zizzbaum Corporation — New combine forced by
    Minna

The Castaways

Characters

Mr. Mulliner
Miss Postlethwaite
Bulstrode Mulliner — Nephew who loves Mabelle. Writer in Hollywood.
Genevieve Bootle
Jacob Z. Schnellenhamer
Mabelle Ridgway — Engaged to Bulstrode
Ed Murgatroyd — Engaged to Genevieve

53a — BLANDINGS CASTLE

First published September 20 1935 by Doubleday Doran, Garden
City, New York, 312 pages. Bound in green cloth, lettered in dark
green. First edition so stated beneath the copyright notice. Identical
with number 53.

First published October 11 1935 by Herbert Jenkins, London, 320 pages. Bound in red cloth, lettered in black. "First Printing 1935" on the verso of the title page.

The novel, the scene of which takes place on a transatlantic liner, continues one of the several plots of *Heavy Weather*. A highlight in Writing a Letter to a Loved One (pp 9-12).

Characters

(9)   (Monty) Montague Bodkin — 28 year old hero who is engaged to Gertrude

(9)   Gertrude Butterwick — Engaged to Monty and on the All English Ladies' Hockey Team

(10)   Ambrose Tennyson — Gertrude's cousin, a novelist supposedly under contract to Superba-Llewellyn and engaged to Lotus Blossom

(11)   Ivor Llewellyn — President of the Superba-Llewellyn Motion Picture Corp. Married ex-star Grayce who wants him to smuggle a necklace into the States.

(12)   (Lottie) Lotus Blossom — A beautiful redheaded movie star under contract to Llewellyn who possesses a dominant personality. Engaged to Ambrose.

(13)   Mabel Spence — Ivor's sister-in-law who is an osteopath in Beverly Hills. Falls in love with Reggie.

(15)   George — Mabel's worthless brother

(23)   (Reggie) Reginald Tennyson — Ambrose's younger brother who loves Mabel

(34)   John G. Butterwick — Gertrude's father and the Tennysons' uncle

(56)   Jane Passenger — Captain of the Hockey Team

(77)   Albert Eustace Peasemarch — 46 year old Bedroom Steward

(134) Wilfred — Lottie's alligator

Places and Things

(11)   Superba-Llewellyn Motion Picture Corporation — Hollywood film company whose President is Ivor Llewellyn

(23)   Drones Club — Reggie and Catsmeat Potter-Pirbright are members

(34)   Butterwick, Price & Mandelbaum — Export and import merchants

160

54a – THE LUCK OF THE BODKINS

First published January 3 1936 by Little, Brown & Co., Boston, 300 pages. Bound in light green cloth, lettered in dark blue. "Published January, 1936" beneath the copyright notice.

Although the plot and characters remain the same, the story has been re-worked for this edition.

First published April 3 1936 by Herbert Jenkins, London, 320 pages. Bound in green cloth, lettered in black. "First Printing 1936" on the verso of the title page.

An outstanding collection of Short stories featuring the classic "Uncle Fred Flits By" and one of Wodehouse's personal favorites, "The Amazing Hat Mystery."

Fate

Characters

Freddie Widgeon — Member of the Drones Club who loves Mavis. His uncle, Lord Blicester, is an old school friend of Mavis' father, Lord Bodsham.

Mavis Peasemarch — Daughter of the 5th Earl of Bodsham

Myra Jennings — Freddie helped her move her suitcase

Mrs. Silvers — Beautiful blonde who wants to divorce her jealous husband, Ed

Tried In The Furnace

Characters

(Barmy) Cyril Fotheringay Phipps — Takes the Village Mothers on their annual outing. In love with Angelica, does a cross-talk act with Pongo.

(Pongo) Reginald Twistleton-Twistleton — Helps out with the School Treat. In love with Angelica, does a cross-talk act with Barmy.

Angelica Briscoe — The Rev.'s daughter engaged to her second cousin

The Rev. P.P. Briscoe — Angelica's father

Briscoe — Engaged to Angelica

Places and Things

Maiden Eggesford, Somersetshire — Where action takes place

Bridmouth-on-Sea — Resort near Maiden Eggesford

Messrs. Thrope and Widgery — Grocers in Bridmouth

Goose and Grasshopper — Inn at Maiden Eggesford

Trouble Down At Tudsleigh

Characters

Freddie Widgeon — Loves April
April Carroway — Beautiful girl who likes Tennyson
Prudence Carroway — April's young sister who likes to imitate
    characters from books
Lady Carroway — Friend of Freddie's uncle, Lord Blicester
Captain Bradbury — Member of the Indian Army, in love with
    April

Places and Things

Tudsleigh Court — Lady Carroway's home in Worcestershire
Blue Lion — Inn at Tudsleigh

The Amazing Hat Mystery

Characters

Percy Wimbolt — Large, stout chap who loves Elizabeth and is
    a close friend of Diana's
Nelson Cork — Small, thin fellow who loves Diana and is a close
    friend of Elizabeth's
Elizabeth Bottsworth — Small, dainty girl who gets engaged to
    Nelson
Diana Punter — Statuesque girl who gets engaged to Percy
Jno. Bodmin — World famous hatter, in Vigo Street

Good-Bye To All Cats

Characters

Freddie Widgeon — Hates cats
Dahlia Prenderby — Freddie is in love with her
Sir Mortimer Prenderby — Dahlia's father who loves cats and
    dogs. Freddie hits him with cats.
Biggleswade — Sir Mortimer's butler

Places and Things

Matcham Scratchings — Sir Mortimer's home in Oxfordshire
Lower Smattering-on-the-Wissel — Nearest village to Matcham
    Scratchings

The Luck of The Stiffhams

Characters

(Stiffy) Adolphus Stiffham — Secretary to the Earl, in love with his daughter. Wins money in a crap game in New York City.

Geraldine Spettisbury — The Earl's daughter in love with Stiffy

Ferdinand James Delamere, 6th Earl of Wivelscombe — Geraldine's father

Gascoigne — Lord Wivelscombe's butler

Places

Wivescombe Court — The Earl's home in Upton Snodsbury, Worcestershire

Noblesse Oblige

Characters

Freddie Widgeon — At Cannes with his uncle. Loves Drusilla.

Drusilla — Doesn't like men who smoke, drink or gamble

Lord Blicester — Freddie's uncle

Uncle Fred Flits By

Characters

Pongo Twistleton — Uncle Fred's nephew who makes him pose as Mr. Walkinshaw, a bird clipper, Douglas Roddis, and Percy Frensham in the course of a single afternoon

Frederick, Earl of Ickenham — Pongo's uncle Fred who assumes the identity of the man from the bird shop; Mr. Roddis, owner of the house; and as J.G. Bulstrode, a neighbor

Wilberforce Robinson — Pink chap in love with Julia. Assistant in a jellied eel shop.

Julia Parker — In love with Wilberforce

Connie Parker — Julia's mother

Claude Parker — Julia's henpecked father

Places and Things

Ickenham Hall — Lord Ickenham's home in Ickenham, Hampshire

Mitching Hill — Suburb of London where the action takes place
The Cedars — The house in Mitching Hill

Archibald and The Masses

Characters

Mr. Mulliner
Pint of Bitter, Gin and Angostura, Small Bass, and Light Lager —
Mr. Mulliner's companions
Archibald Mulliner — Nephew who does a great imitation of a
hen laying an egg. Engaged to Aurelia.
Aurelia Cammarleigh — Engaged to Archibald
Meadowes — Archibald's valet

Places and Things

League for the Dawn of Freedom — Meadowes is a member of
this Socialist group
Mottled Earwig – Nightclub
Goose and Gherkin — Pub in Bottleton East
Drones Club — Archibald is a member

The Code of The Mulliners

Characters

Mr. Mulliner
Whiskey Sour, Eggnog, Gin and Ginger, Half of Stout — Mr.
Mulliner's companions
Archibald Mulliner — Engaged to Aurelia
Aurelia Cammarleigh — Engaged to Archibald
Lady (Wilhelmina) Mulliner – Archibald's mother and widow of
the late Sir Sholto, M.V.O.
Sir Rackstraw Cammarleigh — Retired colonial governor
Bagshot — Sir Rackstraw's butler
Yvonne Maltravers — Actress who plays heroines in traveling
melodrama

(276) "She was suspicious. Her gaze, unlike her waist-measurement,
was narrow."

The Fiery Wooing of Mordred

Characters

Mr. Mulliner

Pint of Lager, Small Bass, Whiskey and Splash — Mr. Mulliner's
companions

Miss Postlethwaite

Mordred Mulliner — Nephew who is a poet and loves Annabelle.
Careless with cigarettes.

Annabelle Sprockett-Sprockett — Beautiful girl

Aurelia, Lady Sprockett-Sprockett – Annabelle's mother

Sir Murgatroyd Sprockett-Sprockett — Annabelle's father

Places and Things

Smattering Hall — Sir Murgatroyd's home in Lower Smattering-
on-the-Wissel, Worcestershire

Smattering-cum-Blimpstead-in-the-Vale — Nearest village to the
Hall

166

55a — YOUNG MEN IN SPATS

First published July 24 1936 by Doubleday Doran, Garden City, New York, 298 pages. Bound in light green cloth, lettered in dark green. First edition so stated beneath the copyright notice.

Nine of the eleven stories in number 55 are here, with "Tried in the Furnace" and "Trouble Down at Tudsleigh" omitted. Three new stories in this edition appear for the first time in volume form.

Fate — see 55

The Amazing Hat Mystery — see 55

Good-Bye To All Cats — see 55

The Luck of The Stiffhams — see 55

Noblesse Oblige — see 55

Uncle Fred Flits By — see 55

Archibald and The Masses — see 55

The Code of The Mulliners — see 55

The Fiery Wooing of Mordred — see 55

There's Always Golf!

> *Characters*
>
> Oldest Member
> Clarice Fitch — Large, beautiful romantic African explorer
> Ernest Faraday Plinlimmon — Small, thin Average Adjuster who loves golf and Clarice

The Letter of The Law

> *Characters*
>
> Oldest Member
> Wilmot Byng — Handsome young man who was an impulsive golfer. Loves Gwendoline.

167

Gwendoline Poskitt — Daughter of the First Grave Digger who loves Wilmot

Edward — Poskitt's dog

Joseph Poskitt — One of the Oldest Member's best friends who dislikes Wilmot

Wadsworth Hemmingway — Retired solicitor who is Joseph's rival for the President's Cup

The Wrecking Crew: The First Grave Digger, Old Father Time, The Man with the Hoe, and Consul, the Almost Human

Farewell To Legs

Characters

Oldest Member

Angus McTavish — Loves golf and engaged to Evangeline

Evangeline Brackett

Legs Mortimer — Practical joker and life of the party who tries to steal Evangeline away from Angus

56 – LAUGHING GAS

First published September 25 1936 by Herbert Jenkins, London, 320 pages. Bound in plum cloth, lettered in black. "First Printing 1936" on the verso of the title page.

A sort of humorous science fiction novel with an English peer and a child movie star switching bodies.

Characters

(7)   (Reggie) Reginald John Peter Swithin, 3rd Earl of Havershot – 28 year old Drone who goes to Hollywood, falls in love with a movie star, meets his former fiancee and gets engaged to her

(8)   Joey Cooley – Obnoxious 12 year old child film star

(10)   Horace Plimsoll – Reggie's family lawyer

(11)   (Eggy) Egremont Mannering – Reggie's cousin who is first engaged to Ann, then to Mabel

(16)   Ann Bannister – American newspaper girl to whom Reggie was once engaged. An energetic go-getter who is governess-nurse-maid to Joey.

(16)   April June – Beautiful movie star who makes a play for Reggie

(54)   I.J. Zizzbaum – Reggie's dentist in Beverly Hills

(57)   B.K. Burwash – Joey's dentist who shares offices with Zizzbaum

(62)   Theodore P. Brinkmeyer – Amiable fat boss of the Brinkmeyer-Magnifico Motion Picture Corp.

(62)   Beulah Brinkmeyer – T.P.'s sister who oversees Joey

(91)   Sister Lora Luella Stott – Leader of the Temple of the New Dawn

(92)   Mabel Prescott – Member of the Temple of the New Dawn who gets engaged to Eggy

(133)   Cosmo Booch – Joey's press agent

(134)   Diran Marsupial – Joey's director

(175)   Orlando Flower – Rival child actor with red hair and freckles

(184)   Chaffinch – T.P.'s English butler who thinks he can act

(212)   Tommy Murphy – Former child star whom Joey replaced

(228)   Pomona Wycherley – Reporter who interviews Reggie as he's Joey

Places and Things

(7)   Drones Club — Reggie, Barmy Fotheringay-Phipps and Oofy
        Prosser are members
(22)   Biddleford Castle — Havershot estate in Biddleford, Norfolk
(35)   Garden of the Hesperides — Reggie's cottage in Hollywood
(91)   Temple of the New Dawn — Prohibitionist religious sect
(135)   *Screen Beautiful* — Movie magazine

56a — LAUGHING GAS

First published December 4 1936 by Doubleday Doran, Garden City, New York, 304 pages. Bound in orange cloth, lettered in black. First edition so stated beneath the copyright notice.

Identical with number 56 except the name Brinkmeyer is changed to Brinkwater.

57 – LORD EMSWORTH AND OTHERS

First published March 19 1937 by Herbert Jenkins, London, 320 pages. Bound in red cloth, lettered in black. "First Printing 1937" on the verso of the title page.

An excellent collection of assorted short stories.

The Crime Wave At Blandings

Characters

Clarence, 9th Earl of Emsworth
Angus McAllister – Lord Emsworth's head gardener
Lady Constance Keeble – Lord Emsworth's imperious sister who wants Jane to marry Bertie Roegate
Rupert Baxter – Lord Emsworth's ex-secretary who becomes George's tutor
Beach – Lord Emsworth's butler
George – Lord Bosham's second son and Lord Emsworth's 12 year old grandson who has an airgun
Jane – Lord Emsworth's niece and Charlotte's daughter who loves Abercrombie
Simmons – Lord Emsworth's retiring land agent
George Abercrombie – Gets the post of land agent. Loves Jane.
Herbert, Lord Roegate – Loves Jane

Places and Things

Blandings Castle
The Man With The Missing Toe – Mystery novel
Emsworth Arms
Senior Conservative Club – Lord Emsworth is a member
The Care Of The Pig – Lord Emsworth's favorite book by Whiffle

Buried Treasure

Characters

Mr. Mulliner
Miss Postlethwaite
Whiskey and Splash, Small Bass, Gin and Italian Vermouth – Mr. Mulliner's companions

Brancepeth Mulliner — Nephew who is an artist, in love with Muriel

Lord Bromborough — Has his portrait painted by Brancepeth. Has an enormous moustache called Joyeuse.

Sir Preston Potter, Bart. — Rival moustache grower of Lord Bromborough who named his moustache Love in Idleness

Muriel — Lord Bromborough's daughter in love with Brancepeth

George Phipps — Lord Bromborough's butler

Edwin Potter — Sir Preston's son engaged to Muriel

Places and Things

Angler's Rest

Rumpling Hall — Lord Bromborough's home in Lower Rumpling, Norfolk

Wapleigh Towers — Sir Preston's home in Norfolk

The Letter Of The Law — see 55a

Farewell To Legs — see 55a

There's Always Golf — see 55a

The Masked Troubadour

Characters

Freddie Widgeon

Jos. Waterbury — Small, greasy pianist who accompanies Freddie at an Amateur Night

Lord Blicester — Freddie's rich uncle, the 3rd Earl

Lady Pinfold — Lord Blicester's friend

Dora Pinfold — Lady Pinfold's daughter with whom Freddie is in love

Egbert — Barmy Phipps' cousin at Harrow who is an expert with a slingshot. He also starts trouble in *Cocktail Time*.

Places and Things

Drones Club

Green Goose — Pub in Bottleton East

Blicester Towers — Lord Blicester's home in Blicester Regis

172

Ukridge and The Home From Home

Characters

Corky
Bowles — Corky's landlord
Stanley Featherstonehaugh Ukridge
Julia Ukridge — Stanley's aunt who lives on Wimbledon
    Common
Barter — Julia's butler

Places

The Cedars — Julia's home on Wimbledon Common

The Come-Back of Battling Billson

Characters

Corky
Ukridge — Manages the Battler
(Battling) Wilberforce Billson — Heavyweight engaged to Flossie
Flossie Dalrymple — Barmaid at the Blue Anchor
Julia Ukridge
Oakshott — Julia's butler who bets against the Battler

Places

Blue Anchor — Pub in Knightsbridge where Flossie works

The Level Business Head

Characters

(Corky) Corcoran
Ukridge
Baxter — Julia's butler
Julia Ukridge
Angelica Vining — Poetess friend of Julia's

Places

Coach and Horses — Pub in Lewes

57a – CRIME WAVE AT BLANDINGS

First published June 25 1937 by Doubleday Doran, Garden City, New York, 330 pages. Bound in green pictorial cloth, lettered in dark green. First edition so stated beneath the copyright notice.

The Crime Wave At Blandings — see 57

The Medicine Girl — see 47

Buried Treasure — see 57

The Masked Troubadour — see 57

Romance at Droitgate Spa

Characters

Mr. Mulliner
Plain Vichy, Milk and Soda, Small Bass — Mr. Mulliner's companions
Frederick Fitch-Fitch — Distant connection engaged to Annabel who wants to own an antique shop
Major General Sir Aylmer Bastable — Frederick's uncle living in Droitgate who holds his money in trust. Hypochondriac.
Annabel Purvis — A conjurer's assistant who loves Frederick
Mortimer Rackstraw — Conjurer professionally known as The Great Boloni who also loves Annabel
Joe Boffin — Annabel's uncle who has had many illnesses

Places

Podagra Lodge — Sir Aylmer's home in Droitgate

All's Well With Bingo

Characters

Bingo Little — Goes to Monte Carlo to obtain the local color necessary for Rosie's new book
Rosie Little — Bingo's wife, a famous novelist
Oofy Prosser — Drones Club millionaire

Tried In The Furnace — see 55

174

58 — SUMMER MOONSHINE

First published October 8 1937 by Doubleday Doran, Garden City, New York, 326 pages. Bound in yellow pictorial cloth, lettered in green. First edition so stated beneath the copyright notice.

The basic plot of an impecunious baronet anxious to sell his hideous abode to a rich American female was used more effectively in number 51. Sam and the Missing Teeth (pp 224-245) not to be overlooked.

Characters

(1)   Sir Buckstone Abbott — Baronet who rents his home to paying guests. Wants to sell it to the Princess. An ex-big game hunter who wrote an autobiography.

(1)   Elmer Chinnery — American paying guest who is a much divorced millionaire

(2)   (Tubby) Theodore Vanringham — Stout young American who loves Prudence

(2)   Prudence Whittaker — Sir Buckstone's tall, slender and elegant secretary

(4)   (Jane) Imogen Abbott — Sir Buckstone's 20 year old pretty and slim daughter engaged secretly to Adrian but falls in love with Joe

(7)   J. Mortimer Busby — Crooked vanity publisher

(9)   Joe Vanringham — Tubby's lean and hard young brother who worked for Busby. Playwright who loves Jane.

(12)   Heloise, Princess von und zu Dwornitzchek — Joe and Tubby's stepmother who had married a Mr. Spelvin before marrying the late Franklin Vanringham

(14)   Adrian Peake — Gigolo going after the Princess and secretly engaged to Jane

(19)   Alice, Lady Abbott — Sir Buckstone's American wife who is large and unruffled

(20)   Sam Bulpitt — Alice's millionaire brother who is America's champion process server

(76)   John B. Attwater — Proprietor of the Goose and Gander

(114)   Pollen — Buckstone's butler

(161)   James & John — The Abbott spaniels

(213)   Cyril Attwater — J.B.'s young son

Places and Things

(1)   Walsingford Hall — Sir Buckstone's estate in Walsingford Parva, Berkshire
(5)   Widgeon Seven — Jane's car
(7)   *My Sporting Memories* — Sir Buckstone's autobiography
(68)   Goose and Gander — Only inn at Walsingford Parva
(152) *The Angel in the House* — Joe's play
(196) Boles, Boles, Wickett, Widgery and Boles — Sir Buckstone's lawyers in Lincoln's Inn Fields
(245) Blue Boar — Hotel in Walsingford

58a — SUMMER MOONSHINE

First published February 11 1938 by Herbert Jenkins, London, 320 pages. Bound in red cloth, lettered in black. "First Printing 1938" on the verso of the title page. Identical with number 58.

59 – THE CODE OF THE WOOSTERS

First published October 7 1938 by both Doubleday Doran, Garden City, New York, 298 pages, and Herbert Jenkins, London, 320 pages. Doubleday edition bound in yellow pictorial cloth, lettered in blue. The first edition so stated beneath the copyright notice. Jenkins edition bound in green cloth, lettered in black. "First Printing 1938" on the verso of the title page.

The third in the Bertie-Jeeves series. A first-rate sequel to *Right Ho, Jeeves* carrying forward the romance of Gussie and Madeline and beginning another with Stiffy and Stinker.

Characters

(1)   Bertie Wooster – Once won a Choir Boys handicap in cycling, went to Magdalen with Stinker and is a friend of Freddie Threepwood's

(1)   Jeeves – Wants Bertie to go on a round-the-world cruise

(1)   (Gussie) Augustus Fink-Nottle – Newt fancier engaged to Madeline who is normally shy but Jeeves gives him confidence

(1)   Madeline Bassett – Slim, golden-haired daughter of Sir Watkyn engaged to Gussie

(3)   Sir Watkyn Bassett, C.B.E. – Retired Bosher St. magistrate under whom Bertie was fined on Boat Race Night. Tom Travers' rival at collecting antique silver. Engaged to Spode's aunt, Mrs. Wintergreen.

(4)   Dahlia Travers – Bertie's aunt who owns *Milady's Boudoir* and wants the silver Cow Creamer for Tom's collection

(4)   Seppings – Aunt Dahlia's butler

(5)   Anatole – Aunt Dahlia's superb French chef

(5)   Tom Travers – Aunt Dahlia's husband who collects antique silver

(15)   Roderick Spode – Tall, powerful and dominating founder of a Fascist organization who loves Madeline. Also designs and sells fancy ladies underclothes under the name of Eulalie Soeurs.

(26)   (Stiffy) Stephanie Byng – Madeline's small cousin in love with Stinker

(66)   Mrs. Wintergreen – Spode's aunt and widow of Col. H.H. Wintergreen

(75)   The Rev. Aubrey Upjohn – Headmaster at Bertie's first school

(81) Eustace Oates — Policeman of Totleigh-in-the Wold

(82) Bartholomew — Stiffy's Aberdeen Terrier

(89) (Stinker) The Rev. Harold P. Pinker — Large, friendly bungler who is the curate in Totleigh-in-the-Wold. Loves Stiffy and went to Magdalen with Bertie.

(126) Mrs. Spencer Gregson — Bertie's Aunt Agatha

(204) Butterfield — Sir Watkyn's butler

Places and Things

(1) Drones Club — Bertie, Gussie, Bingo Little, Freddie Widgeon, Catsmeat Potter-Pirbright, Barmy Fotheringay-Phipps and Oofy Prosser are members

(6) *Milady's Boudoir* — Aunt Dahlia's weekly woman's magazine

(10) Totleigh Towers — Sir Watkyn's home in Totleigh-in-the-Wold, Gloucestershire

(22) Berkleley Mansion — Bertie's flat in Berkeley Square, London, W. 1

(26) Popgood and Grooly — Publishers of *My Friends The Newts* by Loretta Peabody

(65) Saviours of Britain — Fascist organization founded by Spode, known as The Black Shorts

(125) Junior Ganymede — A club for manservants of which Jeeves is a most illustrious member

60 – UNCLE FRED IN THE SPRINGTIME

First published August 18 1939 by Doubleday Doran, Garden City, New York, 296 pages. Bound in green pictorial cloth, lettered in brown. First edition so stated beneath the copyright notice.

The fifth Blandings Castle novel and the first starring Uncle Fred.

Characters

(1)   Pongo Twistleton – Uncle Fred's nephew reading for the bar

(1)   Horace Pendlebury-Davenport – Pongo's tall and rich friend engaged to Valerie

(1)   Webster – Horace's valet

(2)   Alaric, The Duke of Dunstable – Horace's wealthy and eccentric uncle. Has a nasty temper and thinks everyone is crazy.

(2)   (Uncle Fred) Frederick Altamount Cornwallis Twistleton, 5th Earl of Ickenham – Pongo's uncle who married an American named Jane. Tall, slim and distinguished who is a friend of Gally's.

(3)   Valerie Twistleton – Pongo's tall sister engaged to Horace

(3)   (Mustard) Claude Pott – Short and fat private detective of 50 who had been a silver ring bookie. Uncle Fred set him up in business. Loves to play Persian Monarchs.

(5)   Rupert Baxter – Secretary to the Duke of Dunstable

(5)   (Ricky) Alaric Gilpin – Horace's redheaded muscular cousin who is a poet engaged to Polly. He wants to buy into an onion soup bar. His late father William was a friend of Uncle Fred's.

(6)   Polly Pott – Mustard's pretty 21 year old daughter who taught Horace to dance. Small girl engaged to Ricky.

(17)   Clarence, 9th Earl of Emsworth – Wants to protect the Empress

(23)   George, Lord Bosham – Lord Emsworth's elder son who lives in Hampshire

(24)   Empress of Blandings – Twice winner of the silver medal of the Shropshire Agricultural Show

(32)   Sir Roderick Glossop – Nerve specialist whom Lord Emsworth knew as a boy named Pimples

(35)   Jane, Countess of Ickenham – Uncle Fred's dominating wife

(39)   George Budd – Bookie to whom Pongo owes two hundred pounds

(42)   Coggs – Lord Ickenham's butler

(56)	Bates — The hall porter at the Drones Club
(187)	Ed. Robinson — Cab driver for Market Blandings
(207)	G. Ovens — Proprietor of the Emsworth Arms
(272)	Charles and Henry — Footmen at Blandings
(283)	Cecily — Lord Bosham's wife

Places and Things

(1)	Drones Club — Pongo, Bingo Little, Horace, Oofy Prosser, Catsmeat Potter-Pirbright and Barmy Fotheringay-Phipps are members
(16)	Buffy-Porson — Pongo's two seater
(16)	Ickenham Hall — Uncle Fred's home in Ickenham, Hampshire
(17)	Market Blandings — Prettiest town in Shropshire
(17)	Blandings Castle — Lord Emsworth's home
(69)	Senior Conservative Club — Lord Emsworth is a member
(164)	Emsworth Arms — Inn at Market Blandings which serves the best beer
(197)	Other pubs at Market Blandings: The Wheatsheaf, Waggoner's Rest, Beatle and Wedge, Stitch in Time, Blue Cow, Blue Boar, Blue Dragon and Jolly Cricketers
(216)	Bingley — Horace's car

60a — UNCLE FRED IN THE SPRINGTIME

First published August 25 1939 by Herbert Jenkins, London, 316 pages. Bound in dark red cloth, lettered in gold. "First Printing 1939" on the verso of the title page. Identical with number 60.

61 – EGGS, BEANS AND CRUMPETS

First published April 26 1940 by Herbert Jenkins, London, 288 pages. Bound in pale orange cloth, lettered in black. "First Printing 1940" on the verso of the title page.

A short story collection containing four about Bingo Little, two Mulliner's, and three very fine Ukridge's.

All's Well With Bingo – see 57a

Bingo and The Peke Crisis

Characters

Bingo Little – Becomes the editor of *Wee Tots*
Rosie Little – Bingo's wife who owns six Pekes
Henry Cuthbert Purkiss – Owner of *Wee Tots*
Bagshaw – The Little's butler

Places and Things

Drones Club
Wee Tots – Children's magazine
Boddington and Biggs – A Bond Street firm selling dog supplies
B.B. Tucker – Gents' Hosier and Bespoke Shirt Maker in Bedford Street, Strand

The Editor Regrets

Characters

Bingo Little – Went to the Rev. Upjohn's school as a lad
Rosie Little
Purkiss
Bella Mae Jobson – American authoress of children's stories

Sonny Boy

Characters

Bingo Little
Rosie Little
Algernon Aubrey Little – Bingo's ugly son
Oofy Prosser – The Club's millionaire who falls in love

181

Charles Pikelet — Bingo's bookie who has an ugly child
Corker — Oofy's valet

Things

Drones Club

Anselm Gets His Chance

Characters

Mr. Mulliner
Miss Postlethwaite
Sherry and Angostura, Whiskey and Splash, Stout and Mild,
    Small Bass — Mr. Mulliner's companions
Anselm Mulliner — Cousin Rupert's younger son, a curate in
    love with Myrtle
Myrtle Jellaby — Niece of Sir Leopold secretly engaged to
    Anselm
Sir Leopold Jellaby, O.B.E. — Millionaire philatelist
Joe Beamish — Ex-burglar living in Rising Mattock
The Rev. Sidney Gooch — Anselm's vicar

Places

Rising Mattock — Anselm is the curate in Hampshire

Romance at Droitgate Spa – see 57a

A Bit Of Luck For Mabel

Characters

Stanley Featherstonehaugh Ukridge
Corky
Mabel — With whom Stanley is in love
Julia Ukridge — Stanley's aunt
Sir Aubrey — In the Coldstream Guards. Loves Mabel.

Buttercup Day

Characters

S.F. Ukridge

Julia Ukridge
(Corky) Corcoran
Barter — Julia's butler

Places

Heath House — Aunt Julia's house in Wimbledon Common

Ukridge and The Old Stepper

Characters

Corky
S.F. Ukridge
Sir Edward Bayliss, O.B.E. — Retired wealthy man
Myrtle — Beautiful girl with whom Stanley is in love
Charles Percy Cuthbertson — Stanley's step-uncle from
    Australia who is a scrounger

Places

Journery's End — Julia's cottage in Market Deeping, Sussex

183

61a – EGGS, BEANS AND CRUMPETS

First published May 10 1940 by Doubleday Doran, Garden City, New York, 312 pages. Bound in green pictorial cloth, lettered in dark green. First edition so stated beneath the copyright notice.

Ukridge and The Old Stepper – see 61

A Bit Of Luck For Mabel – see 61

The Level Business Head – see 57

Buttercup Day – see 61

Ukridge And The Home From Home – see 57

The Come-Back Of Battling Billson – see 57

Sonny Boy – see 61

The Editor Regrets – see 61

Bingo And The Peke Crisis – see 61

Trouble Down at Tudsleigh – see 55

Bramley Is So Bracing

Characters

Freddie Widgeon
Mavis Peasemarch – Lord Bodsham's daughter with whom
    Freddie is in love
Lord Bodsham – College friend of Upjohn's
Wilfred Peasemarch – Mavis' younger brother attending St.
    Asaph's

Places and Things

Drones Club – Freddie and Cooden Beach are members
Bramley-on-Sea
St. Asaph's – School run by the Rev. Aubrey Upjohn. Freddie
    went there.

Anselm Gets His Chance — see 61

Scratch Man

Characters

Oldest Member

Harold Pickering — Partner in a publishing house. Loves Troon
  but gets engaged to Agnes.

Troon Rockett — Daughter of Walter, famous golf champion.
  Loves Harold.

Agnes Flack — Amazon golf champ

Sidney McMurdo — Engaged to Agnes

First published October 4 1940 by Herbert Jenkins, London, 256 pages. Bound in dark red cloth, lettered in gold. "First Printing 1940" on the verso of the title page.

Characters

(7)	Mabel Steptoe — Small, wiry and hard, wife of Howard
(8)	(Joss) Jocelyn Parmalee Weatherby — An artist who does the advertising posters for Paramount Hams. A Psmith-type hero who acts as Howard's valet. Loves Sally.
(8)	Sally Fairmile — Small, slight poor relation of Mabel's who is extremely lively. Engaged to Lord Holbeton.
(8)	George, Lord Holbeton — 2nd Baron and son of the late Percy Trotter. Engaged to Sally until he breaks it.
(9)	Howard Steptoe — Smalltime ex-boxer who worked as a movie extra in Hollywood. Married wealthy wife Mabel.
(10)	Beatrice Chavender — Widow of Mrs. Steptoe's brother Otis. Dominating, large woman who leads Mabel to believe she's wealthy. Loved Duff fifteen years ago.
(11)	James Buchanan Duff — Lord Holbeton's American trustee and managing director of Duff and Trotter
(14)	Sidney Chibnall — Butler at Claines Hall
(21)	Daphne Hesseltyne – Duff's secretary
(61)	Vera Pym — Chibnall's fiancee who is a barmaid at the Rose & Crown
(75)	Mrs. Barlow — Housekeeper at Claines Hall
(75)	Mrs. Ellis — Cook at Claines Hall
(88)	Charles — Footman at Claines Hall
(104)	Patricia — Mrs. Chavender's Peke

Places and Things

(7)	Claines Hall — Tudor mansion in Loose Chippings, Sussex
(11)	Duff and Trotter — London's leading provision merchants
(13)	Paramount Hams — Duff's favorite product
(59)	Rose and Crown — Inn at Loose Chippings whose population is 4916
(144)	The Gardenia Tea Shoppe — Loose Chippings

186

62a – QUICK SERVICE

First published November 11 1940 by Doubleday Doran, Garden City, New York, 312 pages. Bound in beige pictorial cloth, lettered in black. First edition so stated beneath the copyright notice. Identical with number 62.

63 – MONEY IN THE BANK

First published January 19 1942 by Doubleday Doran, Garden City, New York, 304 pages. Bound in plum pictorial cloth, lettered in black. First edition so stated beneath the copyright notice.

For the first time we encounter the word for Wodehouse's Psmith-like hero when he describes Jeff as a "buzzer." The part where Lord Uffenham resolves to marry Mrs. Cork comes directly from *The Little Warrior* (number 26) while the episode of Chimp Twist getting caught in Lord Uffenham's room is much like a similar sequence in *Money For Nothing* (number 40).

Characters

(1)	Mr. Shoesmith — Myrtle's father and solicitor
(1)	(Jeff) Geoffrey G. Miller — Young, flippant barrister who writes thrillers. Starts by getting engaged to Myrtle but doesn't love her. Poses as Adair and falls in love with Anne.
(2)	Lionel Green — Clarissa's nephew, an interior decorator whom Jeff hated at private school
(2)	Myrtle Shoesmith — Shoesmith's imperious daughter
(6)	Ma Balsam — Jeff's motherly housekeeper
(6)	Ernest Pennefather — Taxicab driver suiing Tarvin and being represented by Jeff
(6)	Orlo Tarvin — Successful interior decorator who is willing to take Lionel in as a partner
(10)	J. Sheringham Adair — Detective agency pseudonym for Chimp Twist
(11)	Dolly Molloy — Brassy, golden-haired shoplifting wife of Soapy's
(11)	Soapy Molloy — Con man who tries to sell phony oil stocks
(11)	(Chimp) Alexander Twist — Crook who runs a detective agency
(15)	Clarissa Cork — Energetic widow of Wellesley who rented Shipley Hall and runs it as a place for plain living and higher thinking. Lionel's big-game hunting aunt.
(18)	George, Lord Uffenham — 6th Viscount who rented his home to Mrs. Cork and poses as its butler. Hid his and Anne's diamonds but doesn't remember where.
(18)	Cakebread — Lord Uffenham's pseudonym as the Shipley Hall butler

188

| (20) | Anne Benedick — Lord Uffenham's 23 year old niece engaged to Lionel and secretary-companion to Clarissa |
| (20) | Eustace Trumper — Shrimp-like man who loves Clarissa |

Places and Things

(1)	Shoesmith, Shoesmith, Shoesmith and Shoesmith — Law firm of Lincoln's Inn Fields
(3)	Halsey Chambers, Halsey Court — Jeff's flat in London
(14)	Shipley Hall — Lord Uffenham's home in Kent
(85)	Junior Arts Club — Lionel is a member
(103)	*A Woman In The Wilds* — Autobiography of Clarissa Cork
(117)	Stag and Antlers — Inn at Shipley

63a – MONEY IN THE BANK

First published May 27 1946 by Herbert Jenkins, London, 256 pages. Bound in orange cloth, lettered in black. "First Printing" on the verso of the title page. Wyman & Sons, Ltd., were the printers (p. 253). Other existing copies in other bindings stating "First Printing" on the verso are second impressions, some printed in Holland. Identical with number 63.

64 – JOY IN THE MORNING

First published August 22 1946 by Doubleday & Company, Garden City, New York, 282 pages. Bound in grey pictorial cloth, lettered in green, illustrated throughout by Paul Galdone. First edition so stated beneath the copyright notice.

The fourth Bertie-Jeeves novel.

Characters

(1) Bertie Wooster — Formerly engaged to Florence, he finds himself so situated again for awhile

(1) Jeeves

(3) Agatha Worplesdon — Bertie's nasty aunt and wife of Lord Worplesdon. Has son Thomas by a previous marriage.

(3) Percival, Lord Worplesdon — Agatha's second husband and shipping magnate

(3) Florence Craye — Lord Worplesdon's intellectual daughter with a strongly beautiful profile who is engaged to Stilton

(3) Edwin Craye — Lord Worplesdon's young son who is a boy scout

(3) (Boko) George Webster Fittleworth — Bertie's bosom pal who writes fiction and plays. Secretly engaged to Nobby.

(4) (Nobby) Zenobia Hopwood — Lord Worplesdon's ward and Bertie's friend

(5) (Stilton) G. D'arcy Cheesewright — Went to Eton and Oxford with Bertie, is now a Police Constable in Steeple Bumpleigh. Jealous suitor engaged to Florence.

(116) J. Chichester Clam — Managing Director of the Clam Line trying to merge with the Pink Funnel Line

(195) Maple — Lord Worplesdon's butler

Places and Things

(1) Steeple Bumpleigh — Quiet and picturesque hamlet in Hampshire

(3) Bumpleigh Hall — Aunt Agatha's estate in Steeple Bumpleigh

(14) *Spindrift* — Novel by Florence Craye

(16) Bollinger Bar — In Bond Street

(30) Pink Funnel Line — Lord Worplesdon's shipping firm

(31) Drones Club — Bertie, Boko, Freddie Widgeon and Catsmeat Potter-Pirbright are members

(34)   Wee Nooke — Bertie's rented cottage at Steeple Bumpleigh
         which Edwin burns down (shades of 51)
(35)   East Wibley — Market town adjoining Steeple Bumpleigh
(36)   Aspinall's — Bond Street jewellery shop frequented by Aunt
         Agatha
(116)   Clam Line — American shipping firm owned by Chichester Clam

64a – JOY IN THE MORNING

First published June 2 1947 by Herbert Jenkins, London, 256 pages. Bound in orange cloth, lettered in black. "First Printing" on the verso of the title page. Wyman & Sons, Ltd., must be the printers. Identical with number 64.

65 – FULL MOON

First published May 22 1947 by Doubleday & Company, Garden City, New York, 280 pages. Bound in turquoise cloth, lettered in black, illustrated throughout by Paul Galdone. First edition so stated beneath the copyright notice.

The sixth novel about Blandings Castle. Particularly enjoyable is *A Meeting at Midnight* (pp. 82-85).

Characters

(1)	Clarence, 9th Earl of Emsworth – His troublesome sisters include Julia, Constance, Dora and Hermione
(1)	Lady Hermione Wedge – Lord Emsworth's short, fat and dumpy-looking sister who has been married for 24 years
(1)	Veronica Wedge – Lady Hermione's beautiful but dumb 23 year old daughter once engaged to Freddie, in love with Tipton
(1)	Colonel Egbert Wedge – Lady Hermione's husband and Lord Emsworth's brother-in-law
(2)	Empress of Blandings – Twice in successive years the winner in the Fat Pigs Class at the Shropshire Agricultural Show
(4)	Hon. Freddie Threepwood – Lord Emsworth's younger son who is Vice President of Donaldson's Dog Joy and is married to Aggie
(8)	Prudence Garland – Dora's slim, short daughter who loves Blister
(10)	(Gally) Hon. Galahad Threepwood – 57 year old celebrity of English sporting life
(12)	Tipton Plimsoll – Young rich American in love with Veronica. Inherited Tipton's Stores from his late uncle Chet Tipton, who was Gally's friend.
(21)	Dora Garland – Lord Emsworth's tall and stately sister who is the widow of Sir Everard, K.C.B.
(26)	(Blister) William Galahad Lister – Gally's godson, an artist, who paints the Empress's portrait under the name of Landseer. Freddie's friend in love with Prudence.
(37)	Edward Jimpson Murgatroyd – Tipton's doctor in Harley Street
(108)	McAllister – Scottish head gardener at Blandings
(173)	Beach – Butler at Blandings
(202)	Edwin Pott – Lord Emsworth's pigman who has no roof to his mouth

(243)   Charles and Thomas — Footmen at Blandings

Places and Things

(1)   Blandings Castle — Lord Emsworth's estate near Market
        Blandings
(5)   Wiltshire House — Dora's flat on the 4th floor in Grosvenor
        Square
(22)   Donaldson's Dog Joy — Freddie's father-in-law makes this dog
        food in Long Island City
(23)   Peterson's Pup Food — Donaldson's rival
(27)   Mulberry Tree — Pub owned by Blister in Oxford
(31)   Aspinall's — Bond Street jewellers who cleaned Aggie's necklace
(32)   Tipton's Stores — Plimsoll owns these chain stores
(35)   Barribault's Hotel — Tipton stays in this Brook Street hotel
        when in London
(66)   Emsworth Arms — Inn at Market Blandings where the best beer
        is served
(70)   Pig and Whistle — Rupert Street pub where Gally lunched
(72)   Blandings Parva — Hamlet near the castle
(74)   Sugg's Soothine — Patent medicine to reduce the swelling of
        gnat bite
(108)   Smithson's — Rakes and hoes may be purchased in Market
        Blandings
(140)   Senior Conservative Club — Lord Emsworth is a member
(157)   Todd's Tail-Waggers' Tidbits — Another rival to Donaldson's

65a — FULL MOON

First published October 17 1947 by Herbert Jenkins, London, 252
pages. Bound in orange cloth, lettered in black. "First Printing" on the
verso of the title page. Wyman & Sons, Ltd., must be the printers.
Identical with number 65.

66 – SPRING FEVER

First published May 20 1948 by both Doubleday & Company, Garden City, New York, 224 pages, and Herbert Jenkins, London, 256 pages. Doubleday edition bound in reddish-brown decorated cloth, lettered in white, illustrated throughout by Paul Galdone. First edition so stated beneath the copyright notice. Jenkins edition bound in orange cloth, lettered in black. "First Printing" on the verso of the title page. Wyman & Sons, Ltd., must be the printers.

The look-alike idea began with Bream Mortimer looking like a parrot in number 29, continued as Hermione Wedge looked like a cook in number 65, and is here completed as the Earl looks like a butler and the butler looks like an earl.

Characters

(7)   G. Ellery Cobbold — Stout wealthy American businessman who is a distant cousin to Lord Shortlands

(7)   Miss Sharples — Cobbold's secretary

(9)   Claude Percival John Delamere Cobbold, Lord Shortlands — 52 year old 5th Earl who looks like a butler and is poor. Wants to buy a pub and marry his cook.

(10)   (Terry) Lady Teresa Cobbold — Lord Shortland's beautiful young daughter

(11)   Stanwood Cobbold — Ellery's son who loves Eileen

(11)   Eileen Stoker — Film star with whom Stanwood is in love

(13)   Augustus Robb — Stanwood's valet, an ex-burglar who finally finds his old sweetheart, Mrs. Punter

(19)   (Mike) Mycroft Cardinal — American talent agent who loves Terry. A friend of Stanwood's.

(28)   Whiskers — Lord Shortland's dog

(28)   Lady Clare Cobbold — Lord Shortland's middle daughter who gets engaged to Cosmo

(28)   Mrs. Alice Punter — Lord Shortland's cook who is loved by Lord Shortlands and Spink, but marries Robb

(28)   Cosmo Blair — Playwright who becomes engaged to Clare

(28)   Lady Adela Topping — Lord Shortlands' eldest daughter who is forceful and imperious. Married Desborough and rules Beevor Castle.

(30)   Desborough Topping — Lady Adela's small husband in his mid-forties who is an authority on stamps and loves detective stories

194

(32)   Mervyn Spink — Lord Shortlands' handsome and elegant butler. Previous employment included a stint with Ellery in America. Major vice is gambling. Loves Mrs. Punter.

Places and Things

(9)   Beevor Castle, Kent — Lord Shortlands' estate
(187)   Senior Buffers — Club to which Lord Shortlands belongs

67 — UNCLE DYNAMITE

First published October 22 1948 by Herbert Jenkins, London, 252 pages. Bound in orange cloth, lettered in black. "First Printing" on the verso of the title page.

The second Uncle Fred novel containing a fully complex set of plots with a like amount of embarrassing moments.

Characters

(7)   Frederick Altamont Cornwallis, 5th Earl of Ickenham — 60 year old uncle of Pongo's who went to school with Sir Aylmer and Major Plank and was known there as Barmy. Wants Pongo to marry Sally.

(8)   Bill Oakshott — Childhood pal of Pongo's who is shy and loves Hermione

(8)   (Pongo) Reginald G. Twistleton — Lord I's nephew who inherited a pile of money and is engaged to Hermione

(10)   (Mugsy) Sir Aylmer Bostock — Bill's 57 year old uncle, an ex-colonial governor who is running for Parliament

(10)   Hermione Bostock — Sir Aylmer's determined, intellectual daughter whom Bill loves with silent devotion. Engaged to Pongo and writes novels under the name of Gwynneth Gould.

(14)   (Bimbo) Major Brabazon-Plank — Lead an expedition to the Lower Amazon which included Bill

(19)   Coggs — Lord Ickenham's butler

(23)   Sally Painter — Small, pert American sculptress who used to be engaged to Pongo and loves him still

(24)   Otis Painter — Sally's brother who published Sir Aylmer's reminiscences

(32)   Emily, Lady Bostock — Sir Aylmer's devoted wife

(41)   Harold Potter — 28 year old Police Constable engaged to Elsie. Before being transferred to Ashenden Oakshott, he had arrested Pongo and Uncle Fred at the Dog Races in London.

(41)   Elsie Bean — Housemaid at the Manor engaged to Harold

(64)   Mrs. Gooch — Cook at the Manor

(102)   Mrs. Bella Stubbs — Harold's 33 year old sister

(201)   Jno. Humphrey — Landlord of the Bull's Head

Places and Things

(9)   Ashenden Manor — Bill Oakshott's place in Ashenden Oakshott, Hampshire
(16)   Bishop's Ickenham — Hamlet where Lord Ickenham lives
(20)   Drones Club — Pongo is an illustrious member
(31)   Buffy-Porson — Pongo's car
(93)   Ickenham Hall — Uncle Fred's home in Bishop's Ickenham, Hampshire
(97)   The Bull's Head — Inn at Ashenden Oakshott
(173)   Popgood & Grooly — Hermione's publishers (Augustus and Cyril)
(173)   Meriday House — Otis's publishing company
(176)   Ye Panache Presse — Former name of Otis's publishing company

67a — UNCLE DYNAMITE

First published December 3 1948 by Didier, New York, 312 pages. Bound in dark red cloth, lettered in silver, illustrated throughout by Hal McIntosh. Identical with number 67.

68 – THE MATING SEASON

First published September 9 1949 by Herbert Jenkins, London, 248 pages. Bound in orange cloth, lettered in black. "First Printing" on the verso of the title page.

The fifth Bertie-Jeeves novel, and the first appearance of Catsmeat Pirbright. Continues the harrowing romance of Gussie and Madeline (numbers 52, 59) and introduces the romance of Esmond and Corky.

Characters

(7)   (Bertie) Bertram Wilberforce Wooster — Got a Blue in Tennis at Oxford. Nurse Hogg took care of him when a child.

(7)   Jeeves — Has an uncle who is the butler at Deverill Hall

(7)   Agatha, Lady Worplesdon – Bertie's strong and dominating aunt who has a son Thomas

(7)   Thomas Gregson – Aunt Agatha's beastly son

(8)   (Gussie) Augustus Fink-Nottle — Bertie's pal engaged to Madeline but falls in love with Corky

(9)   Esmond Haddock — Wealthy, handsome young man who is dominated by his five aunts. They want him to marry Gertrude and he wants to marry Corky. He writes sonnets.

(9)   Charlie Silversmith — Jeeves' uncle who is the butler at Deverill Hall

(9)   Charlotte Deverill — Esmond's aunt who is slightly deaf

(9)   Emmeline Deverill — Esmond's dotty aunt who talks to herself

(9)   Harriet Deverill — Esmond's aunt

(9)   Myrtle Deverill — Esmond's aunt

(9)   Dame Daphne Winkworth — Strong, dominating Aunt Agatha-ish widow of P.B. Winkworth, the historian. Madeline's Godmother.

(9)   Gertrude Winkworth — Daphne's daughter who is engaged to Catsmeat

(10)   Madeline Bassett — Engaged to Gussie

(12)   (Catsmeat) Claude Cattermole Pirbright — Bertie's pal and schoolchum who is in love with Gertrude. Poses as Meadowes, Bertie's valet.

(12)   (Corky) Cora Pirbright — Catsméat's sister who is a beautiful movie star in Hollywood who is better known as Cora Starr. The Vicar's niece who loves Esmond.

(14)	The Rev. Sidney Pirbright — Cora's uncle and Vicar of King's Deverill
(24)	Sam Goldwyn — Corky's friendly hairy dog
(25)	Ernest Dobbs — Police Constable and village atheist engaged to Queenie
(34)	The Rev. Aubrey Upjohn — Headmaster of Malvern House, where Bertie went to school
(70)	Queenie Silversmith — Charlie's daughter and parlourmaid at the Hall who is first engaged to Dobbs, then to Catsmeat, and finally back to Dobbs
(144)	Hilda Gudgeon — Madeline's athletic girl friend who lives at the Larches, Wimbledon Common. Loves Harold and tennis.
(146)	Percy — Hilda's white wooly dog
(153)	(Beefy) Harold Anstruther — Bertie's chum from Oxford who is a tennis champion and is engaged to Hilda

Places and Things

(7)	Deverill Hall — Esmond's home in King's Deverill, Hampshire
(7)	Bramley-on-Sea — Where Thomas goes to preparatory school
(8)	Haddock's Headache Hokies — Patent medicine owned by Esmond's late father
(13)	Drones Club — Bertie, Catsmeat, Gussie, Pongo and Barmy Phipps are members
(34)	Malvern House — Preparatory school run by the Rev. Aubrey Upjohn at Bramley-on-Sea. Thomas now goes there, Bertie went there when he was 12.
(197)	Goose and Cowslip — Pub in King's Deverill

68a — THE MATING SEASON

First published November 29 1949 by Didier, New York, 290 pages. Bound in dark red cloth, lettered in silver, illustrated throughout by Hal McIntosh. Identical with number 68.

69 — NOTHING SERIOUS

First published July 21 1950 by Herbert Jenkins, London, 256 pages. Bound in yellow-orange cloth, lettered in black. "First Printing" on the verso of the title page.

A diverse collection of short stories featuring assorted Drones, The Oldest Member, and Ukridge.

The Shadow Passes

Characters

Bingo Little — Algernon's father and editor of *Wee Tots*
Rosie Little
Sarah Byles — Bingo's old nanny hired to take care of Algernon
Algernon Aubrey Little — Bingo's baby
Horace Pendlebury Davenport — Dart champion engaged to Valerie
Valerie Twistleton — Pongo's sister engaged to Horace
Oofy Prosser — Wealthy tightwad
Cyril — Valerie's cocker spaniel

Places and Things

Drones Club — Bingo, Horace, Oofy, Barmy Fotheringay Phipps and Catsmeat Potter-Pirbright are members
Wee Tots — Children's magazine owned by P.P. Purkiss
The Nook — Bingo's home in Wimbledon Common

Bramley Is So Bracing — see 61a

Up From The Depths

Characters

Oldest Member
Ambrose Gussett — Local doctor who loves and marries Evangeline
Evangeline Tewkesbury — Tennis player who learns golf
Dwight Messmore — Tennis champ and Ambrose's rival for Evangeline

Feet Of Clay

Characters

Oldest Member — In America
Agnes Flack — Amazon golfer engaged to Sidney
Sidney McMurdo — Golfer who works for an insurance
    company
Captain Jack Fosdyke — Handsome rival for Agnes's hand
Josiah Flack — Agnes's rich uncle
Cora McGuffy Spottsworth — Soupy writer

Places and Things

East Bampton — Resort town
Wapshott Castle — Fosdyke's family seat at Wapshott-on-the-
    Wap, Hants

Excelsior

Characters

Oldest Member
Horace Bewstridge — A poor golfer who loves Vera and kicks the
    Bottses into a chasm
Vera Witherby — Niece of Ponsford Botts
Ponsford Botts — Tells anecdotes in dialect
Lavender Botts — Whimsical novelist
Irwin Botts — Ponsford's young son
Alphonse — The Botts' poodle
R.P. Crumbles — Horace's boss
Sir George Copstone — Owns chain stores throughout England

Places and Things

Novels by Mrs. Botts — *My Chums The Pixies, How To Talk To
    The Flowers, Many Of My Best Friends Are Mosquitoes*
R.P. Crumbles, Inc. — Purveyors of Silver Sardines (The Sardine
    With a Soul)

Rodney Has A Relapse

Characters

Oldest Member

William Bates — Strapping golfer who married Jane

Rodney Spelvin — William's brother-in-law who had been a poet and now writes mysteries. Starts writing poems again, this time for his son.

Anastatia Spelvin — Rodney's wife of seven years, a superb golfer

Timothy Spelvin — Rodney's young son

Braid Bates — William's frank and uninhibited nine year old son

Jane Bates — Good golfer

Joe Stocker — Rodney's rival for the Rabbit's Umbrella

Things

Sneezo — Medicine for hay fever

Tangled Hearts

Characters

Oldest Member

Smallwood Bessemer — A slender confirmed adviser who loves and finally marries Celia

Celia Todd — Loved by Smallwood

Pirbright — Celia's Pekingese

Sidney McMurdo — Second vice-president of a large insurance company

Agnes Flack — Amazon golf champion engaged to Sidney

Things

Jersey City and All Points West Mutual and Co-operative Life and Accident Insurance Company — Of which Sidney is a second vice-president

Birth Of A Salesman

Characters

Lord Emsworth — Staying with Freddie on Long Island for Tipton's wedding. Sells a Sports Encyclopedia for a young lady.

Freddie Threepwood — Lord Emsworth's young son who is a supersalesman for Donaldson's Dog Joy

George Spenlow — Timber king who throws parties for blondes while his wife is away. Freddie's neighbor.

How's That, Umpire?

Characters

Conky Biddle — Handsome, not so bright fellow who hates cricket and loves Clarissa

Everard, Lord Plumpton — Conky's rich uncle who loves cricket

Eustace Davenport-Simms — Cricketer formerly engaged to Clarissa

Clarissa Binstead — Rich American young girl who hates cricket and loves Conky

Things

Marylebone Cricket Club

Success Story

Characters

Corky

S.F. Ukridge — Wants to emcee the Bottleton East boxing nights

George Tupper — Ukridge's school chum in the Foreign Office

Miss Julia Ukridge — Stanley's aunt, a famous novelist

Oakshott — Julia's butler who uses Stanley's scheme to turn the house into a gambling den

Looney Coote — Ukridge's rich old school chum who raids the Cedars

Places and Things

Bottleton East Mammoth Palace of Pugilism

The Cedars — Julia's house in Wimbledon Common

69a – NOTHING SERIOUS

First published May 24 1951 by Doubleday & Company, Garden City, New York, 224 pages. Bound in red cloth, lettered in black. First edition so stated beneath the copyright notice. Identical with number 69.

First published April 18 1951 by Herbert Jenkins, London, 236 pages. Bound in orange cloth, lettered in black. "First Published by... 1951" on the verso of the title page.

This novel is a considerable re-working of *Spring Fever*, set in Hollywood.

Characters

(9)   Mrs. Adela Shannon Cork – Tall, stately owner of the Carmen Flores home in Beverly Hills. Silent film star who is haughty and dominating. Widow of the wealthy Alfred.

(9)   Smedley Cork – Stout, poor brother of Adela's late husband who likes Bill

(10)   James Phipps – Mrs. Cork's English butler who had gone to prison as a safecracker

(13)   (Bill) Wilhelmina Shannon – Adela's breezy, hearty, rugged and genial sister, in her early 40's. Loves Smedley, writing Adela's memoirs and known as the Old Reliable.

(16)   Joe Davenport – Script writer who won a radio jackpot. Worked with Bill on the Superba-Llewellyn lot and loves Kay.

(26)   Kay Shannon – Bill's niece who loves Joe

(55)   Lancelot, Lord Topham – Wealthy English parasite living for the moment at Adela's. She hopes he will marry Kay.

(61)   Jacob Glutz – Head of the Medulla-Oblongata-Glutz movie studio

(173)   Ward – Police sergeant of Beverly Hills

(173)   Bill Morehouse – Patrolman of Beverly Hills

Place

(26)   Purple Chicken – Restaurant in Greenwich Village

70a – THE OLD RELIABLE

First published October 11 1951 by Doubleday & Company, Garden City, New York, 222 pages. Bound in tan cloth, lettered in red. First edition so stated beneath the copyright notice. Identical with number 70.

71 — BARMY IN WONDERLAND

First published April 21 1952 by Herbert Jenkins, London, 224 pages. Bound in red cloth, lettered in black. "First Published...1952" on the verso of the title page.

A novel vividly illustrating Wodehouse's craftsmanship. While the Wodehouse flavor is strongly evident, it is a novelization of George S. Kaufman's only full-length play, *The Butter and Egg Man.* On page 128 Hermione Brimble suddenly becomes Heloise.

Characters

- (7) J.G. Anderson — Owner of the Hotel Washington in Ohio, and the Lakeside Inn at Skeewassett, Maine. Barmy's employer.
- (7) Mervyn Potter — World-famous movie star engaged to Hermione, who breaks it
- (8) (Barmy) Cyril Fotheringay-Phipps — Desk clerk for Anderson. The position was obtained by his uncle, Lord Binghampton, a breeder of Siamese cats. Went to Eton and Oxford, recently inherited wealth. Loves Dinty.
- (40) (Dinty) Eileen Moore — Joe's friendly secretary who loves Barmy
- (47) Tulip — Mervyn's Tanganyikan lion dog
- (55) Hermione Brimble — Mervyn's fiancee, the daughter of the financial magnate, C. Hamilton Brimble
- (57) Bulstrode — The Brimble's English butler
- (64) Joe Lehman — Ex-vaudeville agent now a theatrical producer
- (65) Jack McClure — Lehman's partner
- (70) Fanny Lehman — Joe's wife who was known as Fanita, World's Greatest Juggler
- (70) Gladys Whittaker — Jack's sister-in-law who plays opposite Mervyn in *Sacrifice*
- (112) Oscar Fritchie — Assistant Manager of a hotel who is "show biz" crazy. He is Barmy's partner in the play.
- (137) Cecil Benham — The director of Barmy's play
- (186) J. Bromley Lippincott — Attorney-at-law

Places and Things

- (14) Drones Club — Barmy is a member of the Dover St. club
- (31) Lehmac Productions, Inc. — Theatrical production company

(90)   *Sacrifice* – Barmy backs this play starring Mervyn

(190) Lippincott, Lippincott, Cohn, Mandelbaum and Lippincott – Law firm

71a – ANGEL CAKE

First published May 8 1952 by Doubleday & Company, Garden City, New York, 224 pages. Bound in tan cloth, lettered in green. First edition so stated beneath the copyright notice. A dedication does not appear in the English edition: "To G.S.K., the onlie begetter of these ensuing sonnets." Text identical with number 71.

72 – PIGS HAVE WINGS

First published October 16 1952 by Doubleday & Company, Garden City, New York, 222 pages. Bound in grey cloth, lettered in white. First edition so stated beneath the copyright notice. The last Wodehouse book to be published by Doubleday.

The seventh in the Blandings Castle series. Particularly noteworthy are the episodes concerning Gally on Lord Emsworth's Social Life (pp. 100-103) and Sir Gregory's Love Life and the Pigman (pp. 112-119).

Characters

(9)   Sebastian Beach – Butler at Blandings who helps steal a pig. Maudie's uncle.

(9)   Clarence, Lord Emsworth – 9th Earl who is infatuated with Maudie

(9)   Lady Constance Keeble – Lord Emsworth's dominating sister who is the widow of Joseph

(9)   (Tubby) Sir Gregory Parsloe-Parsloe, Bart. – Lord Emsworth's neighbor

(10) Empress of Blandings – Prize-winning fat pig who does it again for the third time here

(10) Pride of Matchingham – Sir Gregory's fat pig, a rival to the Empress

(10) George Cyril Wellbeloved – Sir Gregory's redheaded pigman, formerly in the employ of Lord Emsworth

(10) (Gally) Hon. Galahad Threepwood – Lord Emsworth's brother

(12) (Penny) Penelope Donaldson– Small, slender, fair-haired American who is in love with Jerry. Freddie Threepwood's sister-in-law.

(13) Orlo, Lord Vosper – Rich, handsome school chum of Jerry's in love with Gloria. Gets engaged to Penny and finally back to Gloria.

(15) Maudie Stubbs – Ex-barmaid at the Criterion known as Maudie Montrose. Beach's niece who owns a detective agency. Poses as Mrs. Bunbury, Mr. Donaldson's friend. Used to be engaged to Tubby and after many years, they come together again.

(16) Monica Simmons – Lord Emsworth's pig girl in charge of the Empress. Sir Gregory's cousin and large daughter of the Vicar.

(17) Herbert Binstead – Sir Gregory's butler

(24)   (Jerry) Gerald Anstruther Vail — A detective story writer in
        love with Penny who wants to start a health resort. His uncle,
        Plug Basham, is Gally's dear friend.
(29)   Lady Dora Garland — Lord Emsworth's sister
(31)   Queen of Matchingham — Sir Gregory's new fat pig, imported
        from Kent
(35)   Gloria Salt — A tennis champion engaged to Sir Gregory.
        Formerly engaged to Jerry and Orlo. Becomes reunited with
        Orlo.
(48)   Bulstrode — Chemist at Market Blandings
(64)   Riggs — Aunt Dora's butler
(79)   Jno. Robinson — Taxicab driver at Market Blandings
(136)   Alfred Voules — Lord Emsworth's chauffeur
(175)   Lancelot Cooper — House agent in Market Blandings
(178)   Constable Evans — Policeman in Market Blandings
(215)   G. Ovens — Proprietor of the Emsworth Arms. Percy is his son.

Places and Things

(9)   Blandings Castle — Lord Emsworth's estate in Market Blandings,
        Salop
(9)   *The Care of the Pig* — Lord Emsworth's favorite book written
        by Whiffle
(10)   Matchingham Hall — Sir Gregory's home at Much Matchingham,
        Salop
(17)   Emsworth Arms — The best of the eleven inns at Market
        Blandings serving beer
(21)   Digby's Day and Night Detectives — Owned and run by Maudie
        Stubbs
(46)   Slimmo — An anti-fat specific
(97)   Pubs in Market Blandings — The Wheatsheaf, Waggoner's Rest,
        Beetle and Wedge, Stitch in Time, Jolly Cricketeers
(136)   *Bridgnorth, Shifnal and Albrighton Argus* (with which is in-
        corporated *The Wheat Growers Intelligencer and Stock
        Breeders Gazetteer*) — Newspaper serving Market Blandings
(175)   Caine and Cooper — House agents in the High Street in Market
        Blandings

72a — PIGS HAVE WINGS

First published October 31 1952 by Herbert Jenkins, London, 224 pages. Bound in red cloth, lettered in black. "First Published... 1952" on the verso of the title page. Except for the last page, identical with number 72.

73 — RING FOR JEEVES

First published April 22 1953 by Herbert Jenkins, London, 224 pages. Bound in red cloth, lettered in black. "First Published. . .1953" on the verso of the title page.

A novelized version of Guy Bolton's play, *Come On, Jeeves.* The sixth Jeeves novel, the only one without Bertie. A common Wodehouse device is to make his characters act or look like their names — hence the jokes on Captain Biggar's name.

Characters

(7)   Rosalinda Banks Bessemer Spottsworth — Wealthy American widow interested in psychical research. Wants to buy Bill's home and is in love with Capt. Biggar.

(10)   Captain Cuthbert Gervase Brabazon-Biggar — White hunter who loves Rosalinda, steals her necklace and returns it. Won a large amount of money from Bill disguised as a bookie who can't pay off.

(10)   Pomona — Mrs. Spottsworth's Pekinese

(10)   (Bill) William Egerton Bamfylde Ossingham Belfry, 9th Earl of Rowcester — Poor but amiable peer who is engaged to Jill. Has a bookie business under the name of Honest Patch Perkins.

(14)   (Moke) Lady Monica Carmoyle — Bill's sister and Sir Roderick's wife

(14)   (Rory) Sir Roderick Carmoyle — Floorwalker at Harrige's. A jolly bumbler who managed to say the wrong things.

(26)   Jill Wyvern — Small, pretty, practical girl engaged to Bill. She is the local veterinarian and daughter of the Chief Constable of the county. Jealous of Mrs. Spottsworth and doesn't want Bill to play the horses.

(32)   Ellen Tallulah French — Bill's housemaid

(32)   Jeeves — Bill's butler whilst Bertie is attending a school to learn the domestic sciences. Also acts as Bill's turfing clerk.

(34)   Mike — Bill's Irish Terrier

(172)   Colonel Aubrey Wyvern — Chief Constable of Southmoltonshire and Jill's short and stout father

(172)   Bulstrode — Col. Wyvern's 16 year old tall and skinny butler

(173)   Evangeline Trelawny — Col. Wyvern's 15 year old cook

(179)   Mrs. Mary Jane Piggott — Bill's superb cook

Places and Things

(7)   Goose and Gherkin — Inn at Southmoltonshire
(10)   Rowcester Abbey — Bill's home
(14)   Harrige's — Department store where Rory works
(37)   Drones Club — Bertie, Bill, Freddie Widgeon, Pongo Twistleton
         and Barmy Fotheringay-Phipps are members
(42)   United Rover Club — Captain Biggar is a member
(83)   Lower Snodsbury — Village next to Rowcester Abbey
(172)   Wyvern Hall — The Colonel's home

Jokes on Biggar

Which is bigger, Capt. Bigger or Mrs. Bigger? Mrs. Bigger, because she became Bigger.
Which is bigger, Mr. Bigger or Mrs. Bigger? Mr. Bigger, because
he's father Bigger.
Which is bigger, Mr. Bigger or his old maid aunt? The old maid
aunt, because, whatever happens, she's always Bigger.
Which is bigger, Mr. Bigger or Master Bigger? Master Bigger, because he's a little bigger.

73a – THE RETURN OF JEEVES

First published April 15 1954 by Simon & Schuster, New York,
220 pages. Bound in tan cloth, dark grey boards, lettered in brown.
"First Printing" beneath the copyright notice.

In addition to the title change this is a reconstructed version of
number 73, Chapter 5 having now become Chapter 1. Altogether a
much tidier version. Rowcester Abbey has become Towcester Abbey;
the 9th Earl of Rowcester has become William Egerton Ossingham
Belfry, 9th Earl of Towcester; and Harrige's has become Harrod's.

74 – BRING ON THE GIRLS

First published October 5 1953 by Simon & Schuster, New York, 280 pages. Bound in green cloth, black boards, lettered and decorated in red and dark green, "First Printing" beneath the copyright notice. Sixteen pages of photographs.

A joint collaboration with Guy Bolton, subtitled "The Improbable Story of Our Life in Musical Comedy, With Pictures To Prove It." Although much of the text is autobiographical, several stories are either fictional or happened to others. An informative and funny book, of interest to musical comedy addicts as well as Wodehousians.

74a – BRING ON THE GIRLS

First published May 21 1954 by Herbert Jenkins, London, 248 pages. Bound in plum cloth, lettered in gold. "First Published in Great Britain. . .1954" on the verso of the title page.

Rewritten and containing a more detailed section on the authors' life in musical comedy in England. The sixteen pages of photographs differ from number 74.

75 — PERFORMING FLEA

First published October 9 1953 by Herbert Jenkins, London, 224 pages. Bound in blue cloth, lettered in gold. "First Published. . .1953" on the verso of the title page.

Subtitled "A Self-Portrait in Letters by P.G. Wodehouse, With an Introduction and Additional Notes by W. Townend." Together with numbers 74 and 74a, the most important book about Wodehouse. Wodehouse rewrote and polished many of the letters. Townend's comments add substantially to the interest.

75a — AUTHOR! AUTHOR!

First published June 20 1962 by Simon & Schuster, New York, 192 pages. Bound in yellow cloth, yellow boards, lettered in red. "First Printing" on the verso of the title page.

An extensively revised version of number 75, with new material. Hardly anything is left of Townend's comments, Wodehouse having substituted his own. Dates of letters have been greatly altered. Many of Wodehouse's comments were originally articles for several magazines, notably *Punch.* Some of the material is also included in number 78a.

76 – JEEVES AND THE FEUDAL SPIRIT

First published October 15 1954 by Herbert Jenkins, London, 224 pages. Bound in red cloth, lettered in black. "First Published. . . 1954" on the verso of the title page.

The seventh Jeeves novel, the sixth with Bertie. Has a definite relationship with the Bertie-Florence-Stilton romance begun in number 64. A more distant relationship with numbers 52 and 59.

Characters

(7) Bertie Wooster – Grew a mustache of which Jeeves disapproves. So do others, including Stilton.

(7) Dahlia Travers – Bertie's father's sister who lives at Brinkley Court. Tries to sell *Milady's Boudoir* to Trotter.

(7) Lemuel Gengulphus Trotter – Aunt Agatha's friend, a newspaper and magazine owner in Liverpool, wants to buy *Milady's Boudoir*

(7) Mrs. Trotter – Aunt Agatha's friend who dominates her husband. Has a son, Percy, by a former marriage.

(7) Jeeves – Had gone on a summer holiday. Acquired knowledge of jewelry from a cousin.

(9) Percy Gorringe – Side-whiskered step-son of Trotter who is trying to produce his dramatization of Florence's novel. Writes mysteries under the name of Rex West which Bertie loves. Wants to marry Florence.

(10) Lady Florence Craye – Tall, beautiful platinum-haired intellectual who tries to educate her former fiance, Bertie. Engaged to Stilton, she breaks it off and winds up with Percy.

(11) Lord Worplesdon – Florence's father and Aunt Agatha's new husband

(12) (Stilton) G. D'Arcy Cheesewright – Florence's fiance, Bertie's schoolmate and enemy, rowed for Eton and Oxford, ex-policeman, jealous of Bertie's apparent pull with Florence and drew Bertie to win the Annual Darts Tournament at the Drones

(22) Joseph – Stilton's uncle who is a magistrate at the Vinton St. police court

(45) Thomas Portarlington Travers – Aunt Dahlia's second husband who collects antique silver

215

(45)   Daphne Dolores Morehead — Famous blonde and beautiful novelist writing in *Milady's Boudoir* who greatly admires Stilton

(45)   Anatole — Aunt Dahlia's superb French chef

(51)   "Ephraim Gadsby" — Bertie's pseudonym when caught in a police raid

(78)   Roderick Spode, Lord Sidcup — Authority on antique silver, jewelry. Sold his store of ladies' underclothing.

(166) Seppings — Butler at Brinkley Court

(192) Worple — Trotter's valet

Places and Things

(7)   Brinkley Court, Worcestershire — Aunt Dahlia's country home. In London, she lives on Charles Street.

(8)   Bognor Regis — Jeeves' vacation spot for shrimping

(8)   3A Berkeley Mansions, London, W.1 — Bertie's flat

(9)   Junior Ganymede — Club for butlers and valets in Curzon Street. Jeeves and Worple are members.

(10)   *Spindrift* — Florence's novel being turned into a play by Percy

(19)   Drones Club — Bertie, Stilton, Freddie Widgeon, Catsmeat Potter-Pirbright and Barmy Fotheringay-Phipps are members

(39)   *The Mystery of the Pink Crayfish* — Mystery novel written by Percy under his pen name, Rex West. He's working on a novelette, *Blood Will Tell.* Bertie loves these mysteries, including *Murder in Mauve, The Case of the Poisoned Doughnut* and *Inspector Biffen Views the Body.*

(42)   The Mottled Oyster — Formerly known as The Feverish Cheese, The Frozen Limit and The Startled Shrimp, it is a night club of which Bertie is a member and he takes Florence there

(45)   *Milady's Boudoir* — Aunt Dahlia's weekly woman's paper

(45)   "What the Well-Dressed Man Is Wearing" — Article Bertie wrote for *Milady's Boudoir*

(68)   Brinkley-cum-Snodsfield-in-the-Marsh — Nearest village to Brinkley Court

(69)   Aspinall's — Aunt Dahlia's jewellers in Bond Street

76a – BERTIE WOOSTER SEES IT THROUGH

First published February 23 1955 by Simon & Schuster, New York, 248 pages. Bound in tan cloth, grey-green boards, lettered in brown and gold. "First Printing" beneath the copyright notice.

Text identical with number 76. In addition to the title change, includes a most amusing dedication, originally an article in *Punch*.

77 — FRENCH LEAVE

First published January 20 1956 by Herbert Jenkins, London, 208 pages. Bound in red cloth, lettered in black. "First Published. . .1955." on the verso of the title page.

Like number 48, the scene is in France. It contains Guy Bolton's idea for an Umbrella Club (p. 30).

Characters

(7)　J. Russell Clutterbuck — Publisher of Winch & Clutterbuck who lives in Bensonburg, Long Island with his third wife. He loves to eat.

(7)　Kate Trent — Eldest daughter of the late playwright Edgar Trent, bought a hen and bee farm in Bensonburg

(7)　Josephine Trent — Prettiest of the Trent girls who loves Henry

(7)　(Terry) Teresa Trent — Youngest sister who loves Jeff and poses as Jo's maid, Fellowes

(8)　Henry Weems — Minor partner in a law firm who loves Jo. Solid and unadventurous.

(16)　Fellowes — The name chosen to represent the maid of the rich Miss Trent

(18)　(Old Nick) Nicolas Jules St. Xavier Auguste, Marquis de Maufringneuse — Jeff's father, a rogue who had married Hermione and winds up as head waiter married to a French cook

(21)　(Jeff) Jefferson, Comte d'Escrignon — Old Nick's son by his first marriage to the American Loretta Ann Potter. Novelist who loves Terry.

(33)　Chester Todd — Amiable rich husband of a famous violinist, Jane Parker. Jeff's friend and Mavis' brother.

(43)　(Butch) Frederick Carpenter — Wealthy American who loves Mavis

(51)　Hermione Pegler — Mavis' aunt and Nick's former wife

(54)　Philippe — Bartender in the Hotel Splendide at Roville

(58)　Mavis Todd — Dumb, obedient and wealthy niece of Hermione's engaged to Butch

(70)　Pierre Alexandre Boissonade — Commissaire of Police at Roville

218

Places and Things

(7)   *Brother Masons* — Farce play by the late Edgar Trent which
         was his only success
(9)   Kelly, Dubinsky, Wix, Weems and Bassinger — Henry's law firm
(17)   Winch and Clutterbuck — American publishing house which
         publishes Jeff's novels
(32)   St. Rocque — Resort in Brittany where scene is laid
(45)   Fizzo — Sparkling table water owned by Butch
(51)   Belinda — Butch's yacht
(54)   Roville-Sur-Mer — Seashore resort where the main action takes
         place

77a — FRENCH LEAVE

First published September 28 1959 by Simon & Schuster, New
York, 216 pages. Bound in light blue cloth, lettered in dark blue,
pictorial design in dark blue and chartreuse. "First Printing" beneath
the copyright notice. Identical with number 77.

78 – AMERICA, I LIKE YOU

First published May 3 1956 by Simon & Schuster, New York, 216 pages. Bound in ivory cloth, grey-blue boards, lettered in red, illustrated by Marc Simont throughout. "First Printing" beneath the copyright notice.

The central theme concerning Wodehouse's feelings about the United States weaves in and around a collection of articles originally appearing in *Punch*. Some of these incorporate slight bits of autobiography.

78a – OVER SEVENTY

First published October 11 1957 by Herbert Jenkins, London, 192 pages. Bound in red cloth, lettered in gold. "First Published... 1957" on the verso of the title page.

Subtitled "An Autobiography With Digressions." There are more pieces of autobiography than in number 78, and it contains considerable additional material. The theme of looking back over the years provides the proper vehicle for the *Punch* articles and other choice stories. Much of the "autobiography" is, however in the same vein as that found in numbers 74 and 75 and is to be taken with a grain of salt.

First published January 18 1957 by Herbert Jenkins, London, 200 pages. Bound in red cloth, lettered in black. "First Published. . .1957" on the verso of the title page.

An intricate plot supports Wodehouse's finest non-series novel. Wodehouse brings together many of his favorite characters in his favorite setting. The central figure, Keggs, has greatly matured and has now become a sort of worldly Beach. In his youth a coarse vulgarian, he is now "one of the boys." While Bill technically ranks as a buzzer, he is not of the Psmith-like variety, but is a most refreshing fellow.

Characters

(7)   J.J. Bunyan — American multi-millionaire
(7)   Mortimer Bayliss — Unpopular curator of the Bunyan Picture Collection, with a heart of gold
(7)   Augustus Keggs — A retired butler who worked for Bunyan and Lord Uffenham. His sister Flossie, is Mrs. Wilberforce Billson, the Battler's wife. Currently owns three houses in Valley Fields.
(15)   Jane Benedick — Lord Uffenham's pretty, small niece whose sister Anne married Jeff Miller and went to America. Engaged first to Stanhope and then to Bill.
(15)   George, 6th Viscount Uffenham — Jane's amiable uncle; a wonderful character
(16)   Roscoe Bunyan — J.J.'s repulsive 31 year old son; a fat millionaire, he becomes engaged to Emma
(17)   Emma Billson — Keggs' niece who acts under the name of Elaine Dawn (For her parents, see 33 and 57)
(20)   Skidmore — Roscoe's butler at Shipley
(25)   Stanhope Twine — Unpopular sculptor living at Peacehaven
(25)   George — Lord Uffenham's bulldog
(26)   Leonard Gish — Owner of the Gish Gallery and interested in selling Lord Uffenham's paintings
(43)   (Bill) William Quackenbush Hollister — American with ginger-colored hair who works for the Gish Gallery. Loves Jane and is in competition with Roscoe for the tontine.
(44)   Percy Pilbeam — Owner of the Argus Enquiry Agency whom Roscoe employs to retrieve his letters from Emma
(48)   Miss Elphinstone — Gish's receptionist

221

Places and Things

(13)   Valley Fields — London suburb
(13)   *South London Argus* — The Valley Fields newspaper
(14)   Castlewood, Mulberry Grove — Home owned by Keggs which
          lies off Rosendal Road
(16)   Shipley Hall — Lord Uffenham's estate rented by Roscoe
(18)   Green Lion — Pub on Rosendale Road, Valley Fields
(22)   Other homes owned by Keggs — Peacehaven and The Nook
(199) The Mausoleum Club — Lord Uffenham is a member

79a — THE BUTLER DID IT

First published January 28 1957 by Simon & Schuster, New York, 218 pages. Bound in green cloth, black boards, lettered in silver. "First Printing" beneath the copyright notice. Except for the title, identical with number 79.

80 – COCKTAIL TIME

First published June 20 1958 by Herbert Jenkins, London, 224 pages. Bound in red cloth, lettered in black. "First Published. . .1958" on the verso of the title page.

The third Uncle Fred novel.

Characters

(7)	Pongo Twistleton
(7)	(Uncle Fred) Frederick Altamont Cornwallis Twistleton, 5th Earl of Ickenham — Married to Lady Jane
(7)	(Johnny) Jonathan Twistleton Pearce — Lord Ickenham's godson who owns Hammer Hall and Hammer Lodge. Troubled by his Nannie, an impecunious mystery writer who is engaged to Bunny.
(11)	(Beefy) **Sir Raymond Bastable** — Uncle Fred's wife's half brother who is an eminent barrister. Pompous and arrogant, he wants to run for Parliament. Rented Hammer Lodge and wrote *Cocktail Time* under the name of Richard Blunt. Finally gets engaged to Barbara.
(13)	Cosmo Wisdom — Sir Raymond's nephew who poses as the author of *Cocktail Time*
(13)	Albert Peasemarch — Sir Raymond's short, fat butler who is easily muddled but friendly. An ex-steward who fought with Uncle Fred during the war. Loves Phoebe.
(13)	Phoebe Wisdom — Cosmo's mother and Sir Raymond's sister
(17)	Barbara Crowe — Beefy's ex-sweetheart who works for the Saxby Literary Agency
(17)	(Bunny) Belinda Farringdon — Engaged to Johnny
(29)	Mr. Prestwick — Senior partner of Alfred Tomkins Ltd.
(39)	Howard Saxby — Literary agent in his 70's
(42)	(Oily) Gordon Carlisle — American con man
(48)	Gertrude Carlisle — Oily's aggressive wife
(60)	Nannie Bruce — Johnny's old nurse who runs the Hall
(61)	Arthur Popworth — Owns and drives the taxicab at Dovetail Hammer
(70)	Cyril McMurdo — Dovetail Hammer's policeman who is engaged to Nannie
(80)	Benjy — Phoebe's cocker spaniel
(149)	Rupert Morrison — Owner of the Beetle and Wedge

Places and Things

(7)   *Cocktail Time* — Sir Raymond's novel published by Alfred Tomkins Ltd.

(7)   Drones Club — Pongo and Barmy Phipps are members

(7)   Hammer Lodge — Guest house owned by Johnny

(11)   Demosthenes Club — Located across the street from the Drones Club, Sir Raymond, Howard Saxby and Sir Roderick Glossop are members

(17)   Edgar Saxby and Sons — Literary Agents

(27)   Alfred Tomkins Ltd. — Publishers of *Cocktail Time*

(29)   Ebenezer Flapton and Sons — Printers of Worcester and London to Alfred Tomkins Ltd.

(61)   Blue Boar — Pub at Dovetail Hammer

(61)   Beetle and Wedge — Pub at Dovetail Hammer

(65)   Hammer Hall — Johnny's home at Dovetail Hammer, Berkshire

(108)   Superba-Llewellyn — Movie studio interested in *Cocktail Time*

80a – COCKTAIL TIME

First published July 24 1958 by Simon & Schuster, New York, 220 pages. Bound in pink cloth, black boards, lettered in green and black. "First Printing" on the verso of the title page. Identical with number 80.

First published April 13 1959 by Simon & Schuster, New York, 216 pages. Bound in white cloth, greenish grey boards, lettered in pink and black. "First Printing" beneath the copyright notice.

A collection of short stories, three re-written from other collections.

Big Business

Characters

Mr. Mulliner
Small Bass, Light Lager – Mr. Mulliner's companions
Reginald Mulliner – Nephew who inherits money and sings "Old Man River"
Amanda Biffen – Loves Reginald
Sir Jasper Todd – Amanda's rich uncle and guardian who sells Reggie some stock
Percy, Lord Knubble of Knopp – Lives at Knubble Towers and loves Amanda
Popjoy – Police Constable of Lower Smattering

Places and Things

Wissel Hall – Sir Jasper's home in Lower-Smattering-in-the-Wissel, Worcestershire
Watson, Watson, Watson, Watson and Watson – Law firm in Lincoln's Inn Fields

Scratch Man – see 61a

Name changes John for Walter, and Merion for Troon Rockett

The Right Approach

Characters

Mr. Mulliner
Whiskey and Splash, Draught Ale – Mr. Mulliner's companions
Miss Postlethwaite
Augustus Mulliner – Nephew who loves Hermione
Hermione Brimble – Her late father was the Bishop of Stortford
Beatrice Gudgeon – Hermione's aunt

Oswald Stoker — Aunt Beatrice's step-son who writes novels
Russell Clutterbuck — Oswald's American publisher
Staniforth — Aunt Beatrice's butler

Places and Things

Balmoral — Aunt Beatrice's home on Wimbledon Common
Winch and Clutterbuck — American publishing firm

The Word In Season

Characters

Bingo Little — Editor of *Wee Tots* and writes a story for it
Algernon Aubrey Little — Bingo's baby
Henry Cuthbert Purkiss — Proprietor of *Wee Tots*
Rosie Little — Bingo's wife
(Oofy) Alexander Prosser — Sort of engaged to Mabel and wants
    to oil out of it
Mabel Murgatroyd — Redhead who dates Oofy
Julia Purkiss — Henry's wife and Rosie's school friend

The Fat Of The Land

Characters

Freddie Fortescue Widgeon — He introduced the Fat Uncles
    Contest
Rodney, Lord Blicester — Freddie's fat rich uncle
McGarry — Bartender at the Drones Club who is the official
    weigher
Oofy Prosser — Club millionaire
Horace Prosser — Oofy's fat distant cousin from the Argentine

Places and Things

Drones Club — Freddie, Oofy, Bingo, Catsmeat Potter-Pirbright,
    Barmy Phipps, Percy Wimbush, Nelson Cork and Archibald
    Mulliner are members
Hollrock Manor — Reducing clinic in Hertfordshire

Leave It To Algy

Characters

Henry Cuthbert Purkiss — Proprietor of *Wee Tots*
Mrs. Purkiss
Oofy Prosser
Wally Judd — American cartoonist of Dauntless Desmond who
   wants to use Algy as a model
Bingo Little
Rosie Little
Algernon Aubrey Little — Bingo's ugly son

Places and Things

Bramley-on-Sea — Vacation resort area

Joy Bells For Walter

(This is a rewrite of **Ordeal By Golf (28)** and **Excelsior (69)**)

Characters

Oldest Member
Walter Judson — Golfer engaged to Angela. Loses temper when
   playing golf.
Angela Pirbright — Tennis player engaged to Walter
Mrs. Lavender Botts — Angela's aunt who writes about pixies
Ponsford Botts — Tells dialect stories
Cosmo Botts — Book reviewer
George Potter — Plays Walter for the President's Cup
Mabel Case — George's fiancee

Unpleasantness At Kozy Kot

(This is a rewrite which has a nice twist of **Helping Freddie (23)** and
Fixing It For Freddie (35))

Characters

(Biffy) Dudley Wix-Biffen — Member of the Drones Club who
   loved Clarissa
Clarissa Boote — Broke off with Dudley
Colonel Anstruther Boote, D.S.O. — Clarissa's father

227

Joe Peabody — American TV writer of soap operas and friend of the Crumpet. Marries Clarissa.

Catherine Jipson — 4th daughter of the Rev. B.J., of Piggleston, Hants. Nursemaid of Lancelot. Marries Dudley.

Lancelot Hibbs — Kid whose sister has the measles and stays with Dudley

Places and Things

Drones Club

Simla Lodge — Col. Boote's home at Wimbledon Common

Kozy Kot — The Crumpet's aunt's bungalow at Marvis Bay, Devonshire

Freddie, Oofy and The Beef Trust

Characters

Freddie Widgeon

Oofy Prosser — Buys two wrestlers for matches, gets engaged to Myrtle and buys out

(Jas) James Waterbury — The Greasy Bird who gets Oofy involved with the wrestlers and his niece

Porky Jupp — Professional wrestler

Plug Bosher — Professional wrestler

Myrtle Cootes — Waterbury's niece who cooked for the wrestlers and gets engaged to Oofy

Jeeves Makes An Omelet

(This is a rewrite of **Doing Clarence A Bit Of Good** — see 22a)

Characters

Bertie Wooster — Asked to steal the *Fothergill Venus*

Jeeves

Dahlia Travers — Wants Cornelia to write for *Milady's Boudoir*

Cornelia Fothergill — Novelist of romantic goo

Thomas Portarlington Travers — Dahlia's rich husband

Everard Fothergill — Cornelia's husband, an artist

Edward Fothergill — Everard's father, an amateur artist who painted the *Fothergill Venus*

Places and Things

Marsham Manor — Everard's home in Marsham-in-the-Vale, Hampshire

Milady's Boudoir — Aunt Dahlia's magazine for women

81a – A FEW QUICK ONES

First published June 26 1959 by Herbert Jenkins, London, 208 pages. Bound in red cloth, lettered in black. "First Published. . .1959" on the verso of the title page.

The Fat Of The Land – see 81

Scratch Man – see 61a

> Name change from Walter to John Rockett

The Right Approach – see 81

Jeeves Makes An Omelette – see 81

The Word In Season – see 81

Big Business – see 81

Leave It To Algy – see 81

Joy Bells For Walter – see 81

A Tithe For Charity

> *Characters*
>
> S.F. Ukridge – Tries to give three shillings away and gave one to Horace
> Corky
> Julia Ukridge – Stanley's wealthy aunt who writes novels
> Barter – Julia's butler
> Horace Wanklyn – Eminent novelist who Corky interviewed and whose son Stanley is to tutor
> Patricia – Horace's sister
>
> *Places and Things*
>
> Senior Conservative Club – Horace is a member
> Pen and Ink Club – Both Julia and Horace are members

Oofy, Freddie and The Beef Trust – see 81

82 – HOW RIGHT YOU ARE, JEEVES

First published April 4 1960 by Simon & Schuster, New York, 184 pages. Bound in white cloth, orange and white decorated boards, lettered in black. "First Printing" beneath the copyright notice.

The eighth Jeeves novel, harking back to "Jeeves and the Yuletide Spirit" (see number 43). Bobbie Wickham and the 18th Century Cow-creamer of Uncle Tom's (see number 59) is also a dominant theme.

Characters

(1)   Jeeves – Vacationing at Herne Bay for the shrimps but rallies round

(1)   (Bertie) Bertram Wilberforce Wooster – Attended Malvern House and gets engaged to Bobbie

(1)   (Kipper) Reginald Herring – Old chum who attended Malvern House with Bertie

(1)   Aubrey Upjohn, M.A. – Retired headmaster of Malvern House who is running as the Conservative candidate for Market Blandings. Wrote a book about prep schools.

(2)   Dahlia Travers – Bertie's good aunt

(2)   Sir Roderick Glossop – Eminent brain specialist posing as Aunt Dahlia's butler

(3)   Seppings – Butler at Brinkley Court on vacation at Bognor Regis

(4)   Anatole – Aunt Dahlia's superb French chef

(4)   Thomas Portarlington Travers – Aunt Dahlia's lumbago-ridden husband who collects antique silver

(5)   Homer Cream – American business tycoon

(5)   Adela Cream – Writes mystery stories

(5)   (Willie) Wilbert Cream – Handsome son of the Creams who teaches romance languages at a university in America and who collects antique silver. Is mistaken for his brother Wilfred, a kleptomaniac known as Broadway Willie.

(6)   (Bobbie) Roberta Wickham – Redheaded beauty who is fond of playing pranks and getting Bertie involved with them. Although engaged to Bertie, she loves Kipper.

(8)   Phyllis Mills – Upjohn's pretty stepdaughter who talks baby-talk. She is wanted to marry Willie.

(17) Lady Wickham – Bobbie's mother, widow of Sir Cuthbert

(22) Poppet – Phyllis' dachshund

(29)	Bonzo Travers — Aunt Dahlia's son
(43)	Swordfish — Sir Roderick's pseudonym as Aunt Dahlia's butler
(66)	Augustus — Large black cat at Brinkley Court

Places and Things

(1)	Malvern House — Preparatory school where Bertie and Kipper went when it was run by Upjohn. Located at Bramley-on-Sea.
(2)	Brinkley Court — Aunt Dahlia's estate at Market Snodsbury, Worcestershire
(2)	*Thursday Review* — Literary weekly journal where Kipper works
(7)	Skeldings Hall — Home of Bobbie and Lady Wickham in Hertfordshire
(33)	Drones Club — Bertie and Catsmeat Potter-Pirbright are members
(44)	*Blackness At Night* — Mystery novel by Adela Cream
(69)	*Murder At Mistleigh Manor, Three Dead On Tuesday, Excuse My Gat* and *Guess Who* — Mystery stories read by Bertie
(84)	Bull and Bush — Inn at Market Snodsbury
(105)	The Fox and Goose — A wayside pub

82a – JEEVES IN THE OFFING

First published August 12 1960 by Herbert Jenkins, London, 208 pages. Bound in red cloth, lettered in gold. "First Published. . .1960" on the verso of the title page. In the first issue of the first edition the half-title reads A Few Quick Ones. The second issue carries a corrected half-title. Except for the title, identical with number 82.

83 – THE ICE IN THE BEDROOM

First published February 2 1961 by Simon & Schuster, New York, 250 pages. Bound in black cloth, black boards, lettered in white, yellow, and red. "First Printing" beneath the copyright notice.

Characters

(1)   Percy Cornelius — House agent in Valley Fields who is writing the history of this suburb of London. Inherits millions from his black-sheep brother. An ardent fan of Leila Yorke's.

(1)   (Freddie) Frederick Fotheringay Widgeon — Currently working for Shoesmith but wants to marry Sally and go to Kenya to help run a coffee plantation

(2)   Rodney, Lord Blicester — Freddie's uncle

(2)   John Shoesmith — Solicitor for whom Freddie works and Oofy's father-in-law

(2)   (Oofy) Alexander Prosser — Millionaire who owns most of Popgood and Grooly who married Myrtle

(4)   Leila Yorke — Novelist of romances who wants to write one of stark realism. A large woman in her mid-forties who used to be engaged to Rodney. Married Joe Bishop and left him. Gets him back at the end. Real name is Elizabeth Binns.

(7)   (Soapy) Thomas G. Molloy — American con man selling oil stocks

(12) Sally Foster — Leila's secretary who has copper colored hair. Loves Freddie.

(13) Myrtle Prosser — Oofy's wife and Shoesmith's daughter

(23) George — Policeman in Valley Fields who went to Oxford. A beefy chap with red hair engaged to Jennifer Tibbett. Also Freddie's cousin.

(29) Joe Bishop — Small time actor, now a waiter, separated from Leila and lived with his mother, a former snake-charmer

(38) Dolly Molloy — Soapy's beautiful, blonde wife who got a job as Myrtle's maid and stole her jewels

(39) (Chimp) Twist — Crook who runs the J. Sheringham Adair detective agency

(76) Saxby — Leila's literary agent

232

Places and Things

(1)   Valley Fields — Suburb of London
(1)   The Nook — Mr. Cornelius' rented house, owned by Keggs
(1)   Peacehaven — Rented by Freddie Widgeon, owned by Keggs
(2)   Drones Club — Freddie and Oofy are members
(3)   Claines Hall — Leila's house in Loose Chippings, Sussex
(7)   Castlewood — House next to Peacehaven, owned by Keggs
(7)   Shoesmith, Shoesmith, Shoesmith & Shoesmith — Law firm in
          Lincoln's Inn Fields
(27)   Books by Leila — *For True Love Only, Heather O' the Hills,
          Sweet Jennie Dean*
(63)   Novel by Leila — *Cupid, the Archer*
(75)   Pen and Ink Club — Leila spoke to this literary club
(77)   Popgood and Grooly — Aubrey and Cyril are Leila's publishers
(115)   Demosthenes Club — John Shoesmith is a member
(143)   *South London Argus* — Local newspaper in Valley Fields

83a — ICE IN THE BEDROOM

First published October 15 1961 by Herbert Jenkins, London, 224 pages. Bound in red cloth, lettered in gold. "First Published. . .1961" on the verso of the title page. Except for the title, identical with number 83.

First published October 15 1961 by Simon & Schuster, New York, 220 pages. Bound in lavender-blue cloth, black boards, lettered in white. "First Printing" on the verso of the title page.

The eighth Blandings novel, the second to feature Uncle Fred. Also the fourth Uncle Fred book.

Characters

(5)   Clarence, 9th Earl of Emsworth — 61 year old Old Etonian who loves flowers and the Empress

(5)   Beach — Lord Emsworth's butler for 18 years

(5)   Voules — Lord Emsworth's chauffeur

(5)   Alaric, Duke of Dunstable — Large, stout, bald-headed man who thinks everyone is potty

(5)   George — Lord Emsworth's 12 year old grandson who is interested in moving pictures

(5)   Lady Constance Keeble — Lord Emsworth's dominating sister who is in love with James Schoonmaker

(5)   James Schoonmaker — Wealthy American friend of Connie's who loves her

(5)   Lavender Briggs — Lord Emsworth's current secretary who is tall and haughty. Used to work for Lord Tilbury and wants to start a typewriting agency. Lord Emsworth fires her for wanting to steal the Empress.

(6)   Myra Schoonmaker — Pretty, slim daughter of James who loves Bill

(6)   Empress of Blandings — Lord Emsworth's 3 time winner of the fat pig class

(6)   George Cyril Wellbeloved — Once again Lord Emsworth's pigman

(10) (Stinker) George Pyke, Lord Tilbury — Owner of the Mammoth Publishing Company. Keeps a piggery on his estate in Buckinghamshire and wants the Empress.

(16) Archie Gilpin — Alaric's good looking nephew who works for the Mammoth Publishing Company. An artist who loves Millicent.

(22) Pongo Twistleton — **Uncle Fred's nephew**

234

(22)   (Uncle Fred) Frederick Altamont Cornwallis Twistleton, 5th Earl of Ickenham — A good friend of James and a recent friend of Lord Emsworth who solves all problems at Blandings

(23)   (Bill) The Rev. Cuthbert Bailey — A curate in love with Myra, went to Harrow and Oxford with Pongo, goes to Blandings under the name of Meriwether

(33)   Millicent Rigby — Lord Tilbury's current secretary who loves Archie

(143)   G. Ovens — Proprietor of the Emsworth Arms

(150)   Jno. Robinson — Market Blandings' only cabdriver

(176)   Claude Murphy — Constable in Market Blandings

Places and Things

(5)   Blandings Castle — Lord Emsworth's estate near Market Blandings, Salop

(8)   Goose and Gander — Pub in Market Blandings

(10)   Mammoth Publishing Company — Owned by Lord Tilbury

(19)   Shoesmith, Shoesmith, Shoesmith, & Shoesmith — Lord Emsworth's law firm of Lincoln's Inn Fields

(22)   Drones Club — Pongo is a member

(83)   Cow and Grasshopper — Pub in Market Blandings

(96)   *On The Care Of The Pig* — Lord Emsworth's favorite book on pigs by Whiffle

(139)   Crushed Pansy — The restaurant with a soul

(139)   Flaming Youth Group Center — Lavender went to see "one of those avant-garde plays which bring the scent of boiling cabbage across the footlights and in which the little man in the bowler hat turns out to be God."

(140)   Pubs in Market Blandings — Jolly Cricketers, Wheatsheaf, Waggoners Rest, Beetle and Wedge, Stitch in Time

84a — SERVICE WITH A SMILE

First published August 17 1962 by Herbert Jenkins, London, 192 pages. Bound in red cloth, lettered in gold. "First Published. . .1962" on the verso of the title page. Identical with number 84.

85 – STIFF UPPER LIP, JEEVES

First published March 22 1963 by Simon & Schuster, New York, 224 pages. Bound in grey cloth, grey boards, lettered in dark blue and yellow. "First Printing" beneath the copyright notice.

The ninth Jeeves novel is a direct sequel to number 59, as the Bertie-Madeline-Gussie-Spode romance comes to a conclusion. A clever twist is provided when the Alpine Hat, of which Jeeves disapproves, is used to help Bertie out of a jam.

Characters

(9) Bertie Wooster – Engaged to Madeline and then has it broken
(10) Jeeves – Dislikes Bertie's blue Alpine hat with the pink feather. Poses as Chief Inspector Witherspoon of Scotland Yard.
(10) Dahlia Travers – Bertie's kind aunt
(11) Tom Travers – Collector of objects d'art
(11) Sir Watkyn Bassett – Tom's rival in collecting
(13) Madeline Bassett – Sir Watkyn's daughter engaged to Gussie, then Bertie, and finally to Spode
(13) (Stiffy) Stephanie Byng – Sir Watkyn's niece engaged to Stinker
(13) Bartholomew – Stiffy's Aberdeen Terrier
(13) (Gussie) Augustus Fink-Nottle – Bertie's school chum and newt fancier. First engaged to Madeline, then elopes with Emerald.
(13) Roderick Spode, Lord Sidcup – Loves Madeline and finally winds up engaged to her
(13) (Stinker) The Rev. Harold P. Pinker – Bertie's Oxford chum who is a curate who plays football
(18) Emerald Stoker – Younger sister of Pauline, who is studying painting in London. Becomes Totleigh's cook and elopes with Gussie.
(32) Eustace Oates – Constable in Totleigh-in-the-Wold
(46) Butterfield – Sir Watkyn's butler
(56) Major Plank – Retired explorer who loves Rugby football

Places and Things

(10) Brinkley Court – Aunt Dahlia's residence in Worcestershire
(10) Drones Club – Bertie, Monty Bodkin, Gussie, Pongo Twistleton and Freddie Widgeon are members
(11) Totleigh Towers – Sir Watkyn's estate in Gloucestershire

(25) Totleigh-in-the-Wold — Nearest village to the Towers
(56) Hockley-cum-Meston — Village where Plank lives

85a – STIFF UPPER LIP, JEEVES

First published August 16 1963 by Herbert Jenkins, London, 192 pages. Bound in red cloth, lettered in gold. "First Published. . .1963" on the verso of the title page. Except for the dedication to David Jasen, identical with number 85.

237

86 — BIFFEN'S MILLIONS

First published July 14 1964 by Simon & Schuster, New York, 224 pages. Bound in red-orange cloth, yellow boards decorated in black, lettered in black. "First Printing" beneath the copyright notice. Name on spine is "P.J. Wodehouse."

Wodehouse's artistic level here reached a height which was thoroughly satisfying and acknowledged to be brilliantly executed. Although the idea of helping a friend keep out of trouble for a specific period of time originally occurred in number 34, this is a far superior treatment and altogether highly enjoyable.

Characters

(7)   (Jerry) Gerald Shoesmith — 27 year old editor of *Society Spice*

(19)   (Kay) Katherine Christopher — American journalist who works for the Paris edition of the *Herald Tribune.* Loves Jerry although engaged to Henry.

(23)   (Biff) Edmond Biffen Christopher — Kay's 29 year old brother and bosom pal of Jerry's who is trying to write a novel. He is a drinker who inherits ten million dollars from his godfather, Edmond Biffen Pyke. Loves Linda and marries her.

(33)   Linda Rome — Lord Tilbury's sensible and capable niece in love with Biff. Works for the Gish Galeries.

(34)   Henry Blake-Somerset — Kay's fiance in the British Embassy in Paris

(44)   (Willie) William Albert Pilbeam — Waiter at Barribault's Hotel in Mayfair who lives in Valley Fields. Percy is his son and Gwendolyn is his niece.

(48)   Percy Pilbeam — Ex-editor of *Society Spice* who now runs the Argus Enquiry Agency

(48)   Gwendolyn Gibbs — Lord Tilbury's striking blonde but dumb secretary who loves him

(58)   George Pyke, Lord Tilbury — Short and stout owner of the Mammoth Publishing company in love with Gwendolyn. His late elder brother Edmond, left his money to Biff on the condition that he does not get arrested before his 30th birthday.

(60)   John Shoesmith — Jerry's uncle, a solicitor

(67)   Ivor Llewellyn — Motion picture magnate who advertises in Tilbury's publications

86a — FROZEN ASSETS

First published August 14 1964 by Herbert Jenkins, London, 224 pages. Bound in red cloth, lettered in gold. "First Published. . .1964" on the verso of the title page. Except for the title and the addition of a concluding sentence, identical with number 86.

87 – THE BRINKMANSHIP OF GALAHAD THREEPWOOD

First published January 13 1965 by Simon & Schuster, New York, 224 pages. Bound in yellow cloth, mustard boards with blue decoration, lettered and decorated in blue and gold. "First Printing" beneath the copyright notice.

The ninth Blandings Castle book, a direct sequel to number 65, with references to the subsequent Blandings volumes.

Characters

(11)   Tipton Plimsoll – Tall, thin and wealthy fellow engaged to Veronica

(11)   Wilfred Allsop – Small, fragile and poor English pianist who has to work as music teacher in Dame Daphne's school. Veronica's cousin who gets fired from the school before he starts. Tipton gets him a job in his music publishing firm.

(11)   (Vee) Veronica Wedge – Beautiful but dumb girl engaged to Tipton

(11)   Colonel Egbert Wedge – Veronica's father

(11)   Lady Hermione Wedge – Veronica's dominating mother who looks like a cook. Also Lord Emsworth's sister who lives in Rutland Gate, London, S.W. 7.

(13)   Monica Simmons – Lord Emsworth's amazon pig girl who graduated from an agricultural college. Loves Willie.

(13)   Empress of Blandings – Three-time winner of the Fat Pigs contest

(16)   Officer Garroway – Kind-hearted American policeman

(20)   Clarence, 9th Earl of Emsworth – Won first prize for growing the largest pumpkin and three-time winner of having the fattest pig

(20)   Constance Keeble – Marrying Schoonmaker

(26)   (Gally) Hon. Galahad Threepwood – Lord Emsworth's younger brother

(26)   Jno. Robinson – Owner of the station taxicab at Market Blandings

(26)   Percy Bulstrode – Chemist in Market Blandings

(28)   Huxley Winkworth – Small and repulsive son of Dame Daphne's

(29)   (Sandy) Alexandra Callender – Lord Emsworth's attractive red-headed secretary

240

(31)   Samuel Galahad Bagshott — Son of Gally's friend, Boko, who loves Sandy. Barrister who writes articles and children's stories. Goes to Blandings posing as Augustus Whipple.

(56)   Dame Daphne Littlewood Winkworth — Widow of a historian who runs a fashionable girls' school. Former dater of Lord Emsworth who wants to marry him now.

(72)   Voules — Lord Emsworth's chauffeur

(75)   Marlene Wellbeloved — George Cyril's niece who is the barmaid at the Emsworth Arms

(75)   Evans — Police constable in Market Blandings

(102) Thomas — Footman at Blandings

(105) Augustus Whipple (sic) — Author of Lord Emsworth's favorite book. Until now, he was known as Whiffle.

(129) George Cyril Wellbeloved — Lord Emsworth's former pigman who retired to Wolverhampton and now owns a pub there

(146) Stokes — Footman at Blandings

(176) Morgan — Constable in Market Blandings

Places and Things

(13)   Blandings Castle — Located on the Southern end of the Vale of Blandings

(17)   Drones Club — Tipton, Monty Bodkin, Sam Bagshott, Oofy Prosser and Austin Phelps are members

(18)   Tipton's Stores — America's largest chain of supermarkets, owned by Tipton

(21)   *On The Care of The Pig* — Lord Emsworth's favorite book, written heretofore by Whiffle, now by Augustus Whipple

(21)   Popgood and Grooly — Published *On The Care of The Pig*

(26)   Market Blandings — Nearest village to the Castle

(31)   Halsey Chambers, Halsey Court — Sam lives here, and so did Jeff Miller and Jerry Shoesmith

(31)   Great Swifts — Sam's house near Petworth, Sussex

(40)   Barribault's Hotel — Ultra fancy hotel

(44)   Prosser's Pep Pills — Oofy's father founded the company

(50)   Emsworth Arms — Inn at Market Blandings

(83)   Blandings Parva — Hamlet next to the Castle

(83)   Blue Boar Inn — Located in Blandings Parva

(129) Goose and Gander — Pub in Market Blandings

87a – GALAHAD AT BLANDINGS

First published August 26 1965 by Herbert Jenkins, London, 224 pages. Bound in red cloth, lettered in gold. "First Published. . .1965" on the verso of the title page. Except for the title and dedication to Scott Meredith, identical with number 87.

88 – PLUM PIE

First published September 22 1966 by Herbert Jenkins, London, 288 pages. Bound in plum cloth, lettered in silver. "First Published 1966" on the verso of the title page.

A collection of miscellaneous short stories.

Jeeves and The Greasy Bird

Characters

Bertie Wooster

Jeeves

Sir Roderick Glossop – Nerve specialist engaged to Lady Chuffnell

Dahlia Travers – Bertie's kind aunt, his late father's sister

Percy – Aunt Dahlia's cousin

Blair Eggleston – Angry young novelist who loves Honoria

Myrtle, Lady Chuffnell – Chuffy's aunt engaged to Glossop

(Chuffy) Marmaduke Chuffnell – Bertie's friend

Honoria Glossop – Once engaged to Bertie

Dobson – Glossop's butler

Catsmeat Potter-Pirbright – Leading juvenile actor friend of Bertie's

Jas Waterbury – Theatrical agent

Trixie Waterbury – Waterbury's niece who gets engaged to Bertie to fend off Honoria

Porky Jupp – Wrestler employed by Waterbury

Places and Things

Chuffnell Regis – Chuffy's home

Junior Ganymede – Club for manservants in Curzon Street. Jeeves and Dobson are members.

Drones Club – Bertie is a member

Brinkley Court – Aunt Dahlia's country home

Alsopp and Wilson – Wine Merchants

Sleepy Time

Characters

Cyril Grooly – Junior partner who likes golf and is engaged to Patricia

243

Patricia Binstead — Popgood's secretary engaged to Cyril

Professor Pepperidge Farmer — Author and hypnotist

Agnes Flack — Engaged to Sidney. Wrote a novel and wants Cyril to publish it.

Sidney McMurdo — Golf club champion paired with Cyril for competition

Places and Things

Popgood and Grooly — Madison Avenue book publishers

Paradise Valley — Resort Area

Sleepy Time — Farmer's book on hypnotism

Squashy Hollow — Golf course in Paradise Valley

Sticky Wicket At Blandings

Characters

Freddie Threepwood — Sprains his ankle

(Gally) Galahad Threepwood — Freddie's uncle who also sprains his ankle

Valerie Fanshawe — Beautiful girl who loves Freddie's wife's Alsatian

Beach — Butler at Blandings for 18 years

Lady Constance — Lord Emsworth's sister who wants to get rid of Beach

Lord Emsworth

Places and Things

Blandings Castle — Lord Emsworth's home

Donaldson's Dog Joy — Freddie is vice president in charge of sales for this dog food

Marling Hall — Fanshawe residence near Blandings

Ukridge Starts A Bank Account

Characters

S.F. Ukridge — Sells antique furniture which turns out to belong to Julia

Corky — Ukridge's friend

Julia Ukridge — Stanley's aunt who collects antique furniture

Horace Stout — Julia's ex-butler who stole her antique furniture
Percy Stout — Horace's brother, an ex-silver ring bookie

Places and Things

Rosemary Cottage — Place where furniture was kept near Tunbridge Wells, Kent
The Cedars — Julia's home on Wimbledon Common

Bingo Bans The Bomb

Characters

Bingo Little — Editor of *Wee Tots*
Rosie M. Banks — Bingo's wife
Henry Cuthbert Purkiss — Proprietor of *Wee Tots*
Mabel Murgatroyd — Beautiful redhead who protests the bomb
George Francis Augustus Delamere, 5th Earl of Ippleton — Mabel's father
Freddie Widgeon — Bingo's friend

Stylish Stouts

Characters

Bingo Little
H.C. Purkiss
Aunt Myrtle, Mrs. J.G. Beenstock — Bingo's fat aunt who married fat Sir Hercules Foliot-Foljambe
Wilberforce (Willoughby) — Aunt Myrtle's butler
Catsmeat Potter-Pirbright
McGarry — Bartender at the Drones
Kirk Rockaway — Fat author of children's stories who loves Aunt Myrtle

Places and Things

Drones Club — Bingo and Catsmeat are members
Barribault's Hotel — Possesses a fine restaurant

George and Alfred

(This is a rewrite of **Rallying Round Old George** — see 22a)

Characters

Mr. Mulliner

George Mulliner — Nephew and identical twin. Screen writer in Hollywood.

Alfred Mulliner — Nephew and identical twin. Professional conjurer known as the Great Alfredo.

Jacob Schnellenhamer — Hollywood magnate

Sam Glutz — Jake's rival and friend who was slugged

P.P. Bassinger — George's trustee who squandered all his money

Sergeant Brichoux — Policeman at Monte Carlo

Places and Things

Colossal Exquisite — Jake's studio

Perfecto-Wonderful — Sam's studio

A Good Cigar Is A Smoke

Characters

Lancelot Bingley — Artist engaged to Gladys who smokes cigars

Gladys Wetherby — Poetess

Colonel Francis Pashley-Drake — Ex-big game hunter who lives in Bittleton, Sussex. Gladys' uncle who wants his portrait painted.

Mrs. Potter — Francis' superb cook who hates the smell of cigar smoke

Places and Things

The Crushed Pansy — The restaurant with a Soul

The Explorer's Club — Francis is a member

My Life With Rod and Gun — Written by Francis

Poets Club — Gladys is a member

Life With Freddie

Characters

Bunting — Donaldson's lawyer

Freddie Threepwood

Joe Cardinal — Freddie's friend who works in a bank. Fond of dogs and gets them out of scraps. Loves Dinah.

Dinah Biddle — Arnold's small secretary

Arnold Pinkney — Jane's uncle, owner of Pinkney's Stores who is engaged to Mrs. Cheever

Judson Phipps — Freddie's wealthy friend who wants to avoid Arlene

Julia Cheever — Arnold's fiancee and Judson's sister

Arlene Pinkney — Arnold's athletic daughter

Lana Tuttle — Threepwood's cook

Places and Things

Bunting and Satterthwaite — Law firm in London

Donaldson's Dog Joy

Peterson's Pup Food

Drones Club — Freddie and Judson are members

Time Like An Ever-Rolling Stream

Printer's Error

A Note On Humour

Our Man In America — interspersed between each story

88a — PLUM PIE

First published December 1 1967 by Simon & Schuster, New York, 254 pages. Bound in plum cloth, blue boards, lettered and decorated in silver. "First Printing" beneath the copyright notice.

Contains the identical stories in the same order as number 88, but omits "Our Man in America" and the three articles at the end of number 88.

89 – THE PURLOINED PAPERWEIGHT

First published May 12 1967 by Simon & Schuster, New York, 190 pages. Bound in yellow cloth, blue-grey boards, lettered and decorated in dark blue. "First Printing" beneath the copyright notice.

Contains much from previous books. The main theme of someone wanting to unload his mansion to a millionaire was used in numbers 51, 58, and 66. Ugly but lovable hero used in numbers 56, 65, 66, 84, and 87. Writing under a pseudonym used in numbers 67, 76, and 80. The relationship between Algy and Bill is identical with that of the Biscuit and Berry in number 44. The cat climbing incident (pp. 19-23) came from number 36 (pp. 130-134) and Ferris' disapproving act (pp. 71-73) occurred in number 38 (pp. 148-149).

Characters

(9)   Henry Paradene – Impecunious owner of Ashby Hall. Now in his mid-fifties, he was once in musical comedy on stage.

(9)   Mrs. Makepeace – Paradene's neighbor who cleans house for him

(9)   Jane Martyn – Small, fair-haired heroine who works for the London office of *Newsweek*. Henry's niece who is engaged to Lionel but falls in love with Bill.

(10)   (Algy) Algernon Martyn – Jane's lazy, good natured brother who went to school with Lionel and Bill (see also 26)

(10)   Lionel Green – Handsome interior decorator who is engaged to Jane and wants out

(10)   J. Wendell Stickney – American millionaire related to Paradene. Only son of G.J. Stickney of Stickney's Dairy Products who collects 18th century paperweights.

(14)   (Bill) Thomas Hardy – Algy's school chum who looks like a gangster and writes mystery novels under the name of Adela Bristow; loves Jane

(24)   Clarence Binstead – Ex-musical comedy actor now a Broker's man for Duff and Trotter

(31)   Orlo Tarvin – Lionel's partner

(37)   Mrs. Simmons – Hired cook at Ashby Hall

(40)   Kelly Stickney – Wendell's aunt in her forties who is a delightful character. An ex-chorus girl and widow of Theodore.

(40)   Clarkson – Stickney's 36 year old skinny English valet

(40)   Mrs. Heavenly Rest Johnson – Stickney's nonresident cook

89a – COMPANY FOR HENRY

First published October 26 1967 by Herbert Jenkins, London, 224 pages. Bound in rust colored cloth, lettered in white. "First Published 1967" on the verso of the title page. Except for the title and the dedication to Peter Schwed, identical with number 89.

90 — DO BUTLERS BURGLE BANKS?

First published August 5 1968 by Simon & Schuster, New York, 192 pages. Bound in blue cloth, yellow boards, lettered in gold. "First Printing" beneath the copyright notice.

The crook who repents because of religion was used to greater effect in the Ukridge series with Battling Billson.

Characters

(7)	Charlie Yost — Chicago gunman and safeblower
(7)	Horace Appleby — Stout and baldheaded leader of the Appleby Gang. Poses as a butler and falls in love with Ada.
(7)	Llewellyn (Basher) Evans — Expert safe cracker and member of Appleby's Gang
(7)	(Ferdy the Fly) Ferdinand Ripley — Second story climber and member of Appleby's Gang
(12)	Mike Bond — Slim and wiry owner-manager of Bond's Bank
(12)	Jill Willard — Aunt Isobel's nurse, who loves Mike
(12)	Ada Cootes — Mike's secretary who is short and stocky and a superb cook
(13)	Eustace Coleman — Mike's butler
(14)	J.B. Richards — Financier
(16)	Isobel Bond — Mike's maiden aunt
(27)	Ivy — Parlormaid at Mallow Hall
(46)	Sergeant Claude Potter — Jessop's egotistic brother-in-law employed by Scotland Yard
(53)	Mrs. Davis — Cook at Mallow Hall
(62)	(Smithy) Montgomery Smith — Member of Appleby's Gang
(62)	Frank — An American gangster
(64)	General Sir Frederick Featherstone — A trustee of Bond's Bank
(64)	(Gussie) Augustus Mortlake — A trustee of Bond's Bank
(85)	Superintendent Ernest Jessop — Member of the Wallingford Police
(106)	Sergeant Herbert Brewster — Wallingford policeman who likes Ivy

Places and Things

(7)	Wallingford — Market town in Worcestershire in the Vale of Evesham

(12)   Mallow Hall — Mike's home in Mallow, near Wallingford

(14)   Richards, Price and Gregory — Financial business located in London

(22)   The Copper Kettle — Tea shop in Wallingford

(23)   Mallow — Village two miles from Wallingford

(24)   Norton Court — Sir Rupert Finch's home in Shropshire, burgled by Appleby

(37)   Restharrow — Appleby's home in Croxley Road, Valley Fields, London, S.E. 21

(62)   King's Head — Pub in Wallingford

(104)   The Blue Lion — Inn at Wallingford

(181)   Bodger, Bodger, Bodger & Bodger — Appleby's solicitors

90a — DO BUTLERS BURGLE BANKS?

First published September 19 1968 by Herbert Jenkins, London, 192 pages. Bound in dark green cloth, lettered in silver. "First Published 1968" on the verso of the title page.

Except that Wallingford becomes Wellingford and for a few other similarly minor changes identical with number 90.

First published September 25 1969 by Herbert Jenkins, London, 222 pages. Bound in black cloth, lettered in silver, with "First Published 1969" beneath the copyright notice on the verso of the title page. This is the tenth book in the Blandings Castle series.

Characters

(5)	Lord Emsworth
(5)	Empress of Blandings — Lord Emsworth's prize fat pig
(5)	Beach — Lord Emsworth's butler for 18 years
(6)	Howard Chesney — Freddie Threepwood's American friend who is also a crook
(7)	Mrs. Willoughby — The cook at Blandings Castle
(10)	Lady Constance Schoonmaker (ex-Keeble) – Lord Emsworth's sister now married to the American millionaire, James
(10)	Vanessa Polk — Lady Constance's American friend, an impersonator, who tries to swipe a painting and winds up marrying Wilbur Trout
(17)	Alaric, The Duke of Dunstable — Lady Constance's obnoxious friend who is Linda's uncle
(17)	Galahad Threepwood — Lord Emsworth's brother and Johnny's godfather
(19)	(Johnny) John Stiffy Halliday — Gally's 27 year old godson, a barrister who is good at golf and squash racquets. Engaged to Linda off and on.
(41)	Linda Gilpin — Dunstable's beautiful niece engaged more or less to Johnny
(51)	J.G. Banks — Veterinary Surgeon of Market Blandings who treats the Empress
(62)	Voules — Chauffeur at Blandings
(64)	Wilbur Trout — Wealthy American who had many blonde wives and finally lands Vanessa
(71)	Ma Balsam — Johnny's housekeeper
(73)	Joe Bender — 28 year old co-owner of an Art Gallery in Bond Street
(110)	Jno. Robinson — Sole cab driver of Market Blandings
(159)	Cuthbert Price — Lord Emsworth's pig man

Places and Things

(5)   Blandings Castle
(18) Berkeley Mansions — Gally's flat
(18) Pelican Club — Now defunct club where Gally was a member
(25) Bender Gallery — Picture gallery in Bond Street owned by
      Johnny Halliday and Joe Bender
(34) Market Blandings
(55) Emsworth Arms — Serves the best beer in Market Blandings
(64) Pubs in Market Blandings — Goose & Gander, The Waggoner's
      Rest, The Blue Cow, The Jolly Cricketers, The Wheatsheaf,
      and The Stitch in Time
(70) Halsey Chambers — Johnny's flat in Halsey Court, London
(150) Blandings Parva — Village nearest the Castle
(160) *Pigs At A Glance* — New pig book read by Lord Emsworth
(166) *The Bridgnorth, Shifnal and Albrighton Argus* (with which is
      incorporated *The Wheat Growers' Intelligencer and The
      Stock Breeders' Gazetteer*)
(205) Barribault's — Fine hotel in London

91a — NO NUDES IS GOOD NUDES

First published February 11 1970 by Simon and Schuster, New
York, 220 pages. Bound in orange-brown cloth, orange boards and
lettered in black. "First Printing" beneath the copyright notice.
Except for the title, it is identical with number 91.

SUPPLEMENT

Books written by P. G. Wodehouse
since the original publication
of
**A Bibliography and Reader's Guide to
The First Editions of P. G. Wodehouse**
(*Not Indexed*)

First published October 29th, 1970 by Barrie & Jenkins, London, 192 pages. Bound in royal blue, lettered in gold, with "First published 1970" beneath the copyright notice on the verso of the title page.

Characters

(5)   Homer Pyle – Corporation Lawyer who thinks his sister, Barney, is a kleptomaniac.

(5)   Duane Sottlemeyer – Assistant Manager of Guildenstern's Stores

(6)   Mrs. Bernadette (Barney) Clayborne – Homer's sister, who falls in love with Crispin

(9)   Gerald Godfrey Francis (Jerry) West – Hero cartoonist, golf-loving nephew of Crispin & Willoughby

(9)   Willoughby (Bill) Scrope – Jerry's Uncle Bill, a London lawyer who is a friend of Homer Pyle

(9)   Crispin Scrope – Willoughby's elder brother who owns Mellingham Hall

(11) Jane Hunnicut – Jerry's love-at-first-sight

(14) Johnny Halliday – Lawyer friend of Jerry's

(18) Vera Upshaw – Jerry's spectacularly beautiful, gold-digging fiancée who writes inspirational novels and essays

(19) Dame Flora Faye – Beautiful actress, Vera's mother and relict of the late Charlie Upshaw

(22) Mabel – Receptionist at Scrope, Ashby & Pemberton

(70) Constable Ernest Simms – Mellingham-in-the-Vale's police force

(70) Chippendale – A broker's man who acts as Crispin's butler

(72) Marlene Hibbs – Local girl who gives Chippendale a play to make Constable Simms jealous

(115) Beefy Hibbs – Marlene's uncle and landlord of the Goose and Gander

(115) Buster – Marlene's bull terrier

Places and Things

(5)   Guildenstern's Stores – Madison Avenue, New York
(9)   Mellingham Hall – Crispin Scrope's country house which takes in paying guests

92a — THE GIRL IN BLUE

First published February 22nd, 1971 by Simon and Schuster, New York, 192 pages. Bound in light blue boards, lettered and decorated in silver, with "First printing" beneath the copyright notice.

Identical with number 92.

First published October 15th, 1971 by both Barrie & Jenkins, London, 192 pages, and Simon and Schuster, New York, 192 pages. Barrie & Jenkins edition bound in prussian blue cloth, lettered in gold. "First published 1971" on the verso of the title page. Simon and Schuster edition bound in yellow cloth, lettered in black. "First printing" on the verso of the title page.

Commemorating Plum's 90th birthday, both publishers, in a rare spirit of cooperation, issued this tenth Bertie-Jeeves novel which finally resolves the Bassett-Spode romance, which, as it turned out, was indeed continued from *Stiff Upper Lip, Jeeves*. Note that Barrie & Jenkins called it *Much Obliged, Jeeves*, and that Simon and Schuster entitled it *Jeeves and the Tie That Binds*. This title change necessitated the addition of a few paragraphs at the end of the last chapter to explain this title. Except for minor changes to American-English, the *Market Snodsbury Argus-Intelligencer* for the *Market Snodsbury Argus-Reminder*, it is identical to the Barrie & Jenkins edition.

Page numbering here follows the Barrie & Jenkins edition.

Characters

(5) (Bertie) Bertram Wilberforce Wooster – In trying to help Ginger, he becomes engaged once again and however briefly, to Florence

(5) Jeeves – We learn for the first time that his first name is Reginald

(5) Madeline Bassett – Sir Watkyn's daughter and Spode's fiancée. She, too, was once engaged to Bertie

(5) Roderick Spode, Lord Sidcup – Engaged to Madeline Bassett and ever desirous of spreading Bertie all over the lawn and dancing on him with hob-nailed boots

(12) Rupert Bingley – County member of the Junior Ganymede who, when under the name of Brinkley in No. 51, was Bertie's former manservant. He now lives in affluence in Market Snodsbury with a butler of his own

(13) Dahlia Travers – Bertie's good and deserving Aunt, the sister of his late father. Wants her daughter, Angela, to marry Tuppy Glossop to whom she has been engaged for two years

(15) Anatole – Aunt Dahlia's master chef

(16)   (Ginger) Harold Winship – Bertie's college chum and Market Snodsbury's Conservative candidate for Parliament who lives in Steeple Bumpleigh, Essex. Engaged to Florence Craye

(20)   Florence Craye – Ginger's bossy fiancée who was once engaged to Bertie. Her father is Bertie's Uncle Percy

(24)   Magnolia Glendennon – A secretary from South Carolina living in London, now working for Ginger

(24)   Lady Worplesdon – Bertie's Aunt Agatha who lives in Steeple Bumpleigh

(41)   L. P. Runkle – Fat financier who wants to sell Tom Travers a silver porringer for his silver collection

(48)   Seppings – Aunt Dahlia's butler

(54)   Mrs. McCorkadale – Ginger's opponent in his race for a seat in Parliament. She is also a local barrister

(106)   Bastable – Bingley's butler

Places and Things

(8)   The Junior Ganymede – Jeeves' Curzon Street club for butlers and gentlemen's personal gentlemen

(14)   Market Snodsbury – Market town in Worcestershire

(17)   Barribault's Grillroom – Bertie and Ginger lunch there in London

(19)   Drones Club – Bertie's home-away-from-home. Ginger resigned from it

(57)   Runkle's Magic Midgets – Pills for curing headaches invented by Tuppy Glossop's father who worked for L. P. Runkle

(102)   *Market Snodsbury Argus-Reminder* – Bi-weekly newspaper whose politics are anti-conservative

94 — PEARLS, GIRLS AND MONTY BODKIN

First published October 12th, 1972 by Barrie & Jenkins, London, 192 pages. Bound in green cloth, lettered in gold, with "First published 1972" beneath the copyright notice on the verso of the title page.

This is a direct sequel to *The Luck of the Bodkins*, carrying on the story of Monty's determination to win Gertrude's hand.

Characters

(7)   (Monty) Montrose Bodkin – Adviser for Productions for Superba-Llewellyn motion picture studio. Engaged to Gertrude Butterwick. Becomes Secretary to Ivor Llewellyn in the writing of his autobiography

(7)   (Sandy) Alexandra Miller – Monty's small, pretty and vivacious secretary who loves him

(8)   Gertrude Butterwick – Reggie Tennyson's hockey-playing cousin who lives at 11 Croxted Road, West Dulwich. Monty's fiancée

(9)   (Jumbo) Ivor Llewellyn – President of Superba-Llewellyn

(13)   Grayce Llewellyn – Ivor's domineering 5th and current wife, a former silent screen star and Mavis' mother

(16)   J. B. Butterwick – Gertrude's father, an import-export merchant

(40)   Mavis Mulligan – Grayce's imperious daughter by her first marriage to silent movie star Orlando Mulligan. A tall, handsome girl with a fine figure. Loves Jimmy Ponder

(43)   Chimp Twist – Professionally known as J. Sheringham Adair, Private Investigator. Supposed to be guarding Grayce's pearl necklace, he becomes Ivor's valet

(48)   Soapy Molloy – Con man posing as a rich American with oil interests. Tries to sell stock in non-existent oil wells

(48)   Dolly Molloy – Soapy's wife and professional shop-lifter

(75)   Jimmy Ponder – A Greek god with a small clipped moustache who is a partner in a jewelry firm. Bought oil stock from Soapy and gets engaged to Mavis

(76)   Wilfred Chisholm – Hockey-playing bounder for England who is in love with Gertrude. His full-time occupation is that of a policeman who tries to arrest Monty, with whom he was at school

(90)   Otto Flannery – Owns *The Happy Prawn* nightclub. Married Ivor's third wife, Gloria

261

(7)   Superba-Llewellyn – A motion picture company located at Llewellyn City, California

(9)   Drones Club – Monty Bodkin is a popular and one of two really moneyed members of the Dover Street club

(21)   Barribault's – Posh London hotel where Monty lunched with Sandy

(22)   Butterwick, Price and Mandelbaum – Import and export merchants

(32)   Mellingham Hall – The Llewellyn's rented place in Sussex

(88)   Senior Conservative Club – J. B. Butterwick is a member

(94)   The Happy Prawn – Flannery's nightclub formerly known as The Giddy Goat and The Oo-La-La

(123)   *By Honour Bound* – Novel by Rosie M. Banks which made a profound impression on Monty

94a – THE PLOT THAT THICKENED

First published August 6th, 1973 by Simon and Schuster, New York, 222 pages. Bound in rust cloth, lettered and decorated in gold. Numbers one through ten beneath the copyright notice on the verso of the title page.

Except for the title and the dedication to Sheran (Hornby), this is identical to number 94.

95 – BACHELORS ANONYMOUS

First published October 15th, 1973 by Barrie & Jenkins, London, 192 pages. Bound in green cloth, lettered in gold, with "First published in 1973" on top of the copyright notice on the verso of the title page.

This is a direct sequel to *Pearls, Girls and Monty Bodkin* as it affects Ivor Llewellyn's story.

Characters

(7)   Ephraim Trout – Ivor Llewellyn's long-time lawyer friend, who handled all of his five divorces

(7)   Ivor Llewellyn – Much married and currently divorced head of a motion picture studio, who goes to London again

(11)   Fred Basset – Trout's friend and charter member of Bachelors Anonymous

(12)   Johnny Runcible – Trout's friend and charter member of Bachelors Anonymous

(12)   G. J. Flannery – Trout's friend and charter member of Bachelors Anonymous

(15)   Vera Dalrymple – Leading lady in *Cousin Angela* and handsome brunette who goes after Ivor Llewellyn

(15)   Joseph Pickering – Playwright and amateur middleweight boxing champion in love with Sally Fitch

(16)   (Sally) Sarah Fitch – Pretty journalist for a weekly paper, who, subject to conditions, inherts money

(24)   Sir Jaklyn Warner, Baronet – A louse and cadger engaged to Daphne. Formerly engaged to Sally, and tries to be again when he finds out she inherited money

(32)   Jerry Nichols – Joe's friend who has become a junior partner in his father's law firm of Nichols, Erridge and Trubshaw

(33)   Mabel Potter – Sally's friend and secretary to theatre manager, Edgar Sampson. Engaged to Charlie, a stockbroker

(55)   Daphne Dolby – Detective and owner of an agency. Hired to see that Sally doesn't smoke for two years

(72)   Bosher – Llewellyn's ex-valet

(104)   Cyril Pemberton – Works for Daphne and acts as a witness to her marriage

(110)   Jane Priestley – Sally's old nanny who lives in Valley Fields

(114)   Percy – Mrs. Bingham's dog who likes to chase Jane Priestley's three cats

(121)   Amelia Bingham – Comfortably plump widow and nurse at St.
          Swithin's, who owns the other half of Jane Priestley's
          house. Ephraim Trout falls in love with her

Places and Things

(7)   Trout, Wapshott and Edelstein – Legal firm headed by
          Ephraim Trout
(7)   Superba-Llewellyn Studio – Ivor's motion picture studio
          located in Llewellyn City, Hollywood
(10)   Bachelors Anonymous – A club in Hollywood based on
          Alcoholics Anonymous for bachelors wishing to remain so
(11)   Nichols, Erridge, Trubshaw and Nichols – Law firm in Bedford
          Row, London
(15)   *Cousin Angela* – A comedy in three acts running at the Regal
          Theatre, starring Vera Dalrymple and written by Joe
          Pickering
(38)   Much Middlefold, Worcs. – Sally's hometown
(50)   Barribault's Grillroom – Popular posh restaurant in world-
          famous hotel in London
(53)   Anti-Tobacco League – Beneficiary of Letitia Carberry's will
(55)   Eagle Eye Detective Agency – Owned by Daphne Dolby
(114)   The Laurels – Jane Priestley's house in the Burbage Road,
          Valley Fields

95a – BACHELORS ANONYMOUS

First published August 28th, 1974 by Simon and Schuster, New
York, 190 pages. Bound in blue cloth, lettered and decorated in silver.
Numbers one through ten beneath the copyright notice on the verso of the
title page.

Except for the dedication here to Peter Schwed, and a few minor
additions into American-English, this is identical to number 95.

96 – AUNTS AREN'T GENTLEMEN

First published October 17th, 1974 by Barrie & Jenkins, London, 176 pages. Bound in royal blue cloth, lettered in gold, with "First published in 1974" on top of the copyright notice on the verso of the title page.

This is the eleventh and last Bertie-Jeeves novel, and continues Bertie's life from *Much Obliged, Jeeves/Jeeves and the Tie That Binds*.

Characters

(5)   (Bertie) Bertram Wooster – Once asked Vanessa to marry him, but she turned him down
(5)   Jeeves – One of his aunts lives in Maiden Eggesford
(6)   E. Jimson Murgatroyd – Harley Street physician who treated Bertie's pink spots. An old school chum of Major Plank's
(9)   Vanessa Cook – A radiant beauty who leads protesters. She is engaged to Orlo Porter
(10)   (Orlo) O. J. Porter – Beefy red-headed insurance salesman for the London and Home Counties Insurance Company, who is engaged to Vanessa. Went to Oxford with Bertie, but not chums. Inherited a pile with Mr. Cook as trustee
(14)   Mr. Cook – Vanessa's father and Orlo's trustee. Owns race horses
(17)   Major Plank – Explorer and Rugby football fan. Has recurring bouts of malaria. Guest of Cook's
(21)   Dahlia Travers – Bertie's aunt who wants him to steal a car
(23)   Col. James Briscoe – Aunt Dahlia's friend who owns a racing stable in Maiden Eggesford, Somerset
(44)   The Rev. Ambrose Briscoe – The Colonel's brother
(45)   Angelica Briscoe – The Reverend's daughter
(86)   (Billy) Herbert Graham – King of the poachers who keeps stealing Mr. Cook's cat
(117)   Mrs. P. B. Pigott – Jeeves' aunt living at Balmoral, Mafeking Road, Maiden Eggesford

Places and Things

(28)   The Goose and Grasshopper – Inn at Maiden Eggesford
(29)   Eggesford Court – Home of Mr. Cook

96a – THE CAT-NAPPERS

First published April 14th, 1975 by Simon and Schuster, New York, 192 pages. Bound in brown cloth, lettered in gold, decorated in black. Numbers one through ten beneath the copyright notice on the verso of the title page.

Except for the title, it is identical to number 96.

266

97 – SUNSET AT BLANDINGS

First published November 17th, 1977 by Chatto & Windus, London, 216 pages. Bound in blue boards, lettered in gold with endpapers, two sketches and one drawing by Ionicus, and Notes and Appendices by Richard Usborne.

Incomplete first draft of the eleventh Blandings Castle novel. PGW had typed out the first sixteen chapters and left notes for the remaining six. After finishing the entire plot, he would have then rewritten the novel completely, fleshing it out and changing much of the characters and scenes. Annoying and unnecessary notes are supplied throughout the sixteen chapters by Richard Usborne. After the sixteen chapters, Mr. Usborne then takes us through all of PGW's dated notes for this work, first the plot with alternative suggestions to the end, and then shows us how Plum thought through his plots. With actual reproductions of his notes, and printed notes side by side, it is the most instructive insight we get into how PGW constructed his novels. Usborne is excellent here.

Characters

(11) Sir James Piper – England's Chancellor of the Exchequer
(11) Claude Duff – Sir James' junior secretary whose aunt is Dame Daphne Winkworth. His uncle is the Duff of Duff and Trotter, provision merchants
(11) Brenda Piper – Sir James' forceful spinster sister who rules him
(11) Lady Florence Moresby – One of the many domineering sisters of Lord Emsworth. Also widow of the rich American J. J. Underwood. Currently separated from her second husband, Kevin
(11) Clarence, 9th Earl of Emsworth – Wants to have the Empress's portrait painted
(13) (Vicky) Victoria Underwood – Florence's pretty step-daughter who studied Art in London, and falls in love with Jeff Bennison
(13) Sergeant E. B. Murchison – Scotland Yard detective who acts as bodyguard to Sir James
(14) Lady Diana Phipps – Another of Lord Emsworth's sisters, the only one Galahad likes. She is beautiful, the widow of Rollo, and Sir James was once in love with her

(17)   (Gally) Galahad Threepwood – Clarence's younger brother,
        who used to be good friends with Sir James. Both were
        members of the Pelican Club
(18)   Jno. Robinson – Taxi owner/driver in Market Blandings
(19)   Sebastian Beach – Butler at the Castle who worked there for
        18 years
(19)   Empress of Blandings – 3 time Silver medal winning Berkshire
        sow
(20)   Marilyn Poole – Lady Diana's maid
(26)   (Bingo) Jeff Bennison – An impecunious artist in love with
        Vicky. Teaches drawing at a girls' school in Eastbourne
        owned by Dame Daphne Winkworth. Went to school with
        Claude Duff
(35)   Dame Daphne Winkworth – Fires Jeff as a drawing teacher at
        her school
(68)   Freddie Threepwood – Lord Emsworth's younger son, who
        works and lives in America. Comes to London to drum up
        trade for the English branch of Donaldson's Dog Joy

Places and Things
(11)   Blandings Castle – Shropshire home of the Threepwoods
(22)   Athenaeum – Sir James' club
(43)   Emsworth Arms – Market Blandings' best pub whose celebrated
        beer is brewed by its proprietor, G. Ovens
(58)   Wrykyn – Jeff and Claude were at the school together. They
        shared a study in the same house
(68)   Ritz Hotel – The most expensive hotel in London. Where
        Freddie stayed – on an expense account
(83)   *On the Care of the Pig* – Whiffle's classic and Lord Emsworth's
        favourite book

97a – SUNSET AT BLANDINGS

First published September 7th, 1978 by Simon and Schuster, New
York, 218 pages. Bound in brown-black cloth, lettered and decorated in
white. Numbers one through ten beneath the copyright notice on the
verso of the title page.

Except for a Note To The American Reader, at the end, this is
identical to number 97.

INDEX TO PUBLISHERS AND THEIR TITLES

ANTHOLOGIES

Selected and/or Edited by PGW

Jeeves Omnibus, 1931. Herbert Jenkins, London.
A Century of Humour, 1934. Hutchinson, London.
Mulliner Omnibus, 1935. Herbert Jenkins, London.
Best of Modern Humor, 1952. McBride, New York.
The Week-End Book of Humor, 1952. Washburn, New York.
Selected Stories By P.G. Wodehouse, 1958. Modern Library, New York.
The Most of P.G. Wodehouse, 1960. Simon and Schuster, New York.
A Carnival of Modern Humor, 1967. Delacorte Press, New York.
The World of Jeeves, 1967. Herbert Jenkins, London.
The World of Mr. Mulliner, 1972. Barrie & Jenkins, London.
The Golf Omnibus, 1973. Barrie & Jenkins, London.
The World of Psmith, 1974. Barrie & Jenkins, London.

Containing PGW Stories Only

Nothing But Wodehouse, 1932. Doubleday Doran, Garden City, New York.
Library of Humour: P.G. Wodehouse, 1934. Methuen, London.
Week-End Wodehouse, 1939. Doubleday Doran, Garden City, New York.
Week-End Wodehouse, 1939. Herbert Jenkins, London.
Wodehouse On Golf, 1940. Doubleday Doran, Garden City, New York.
The Best of Wodehouse, 1949. Pocket Books, New York.
The World of Ukridge, 1975. Barrie & Jenkins, London
The World of Blandings, 1976. Barrie & Jenkins, London
Jeeves, Jeeves, Jeeves, 1976. Avon, New York.
The Uncollected Wodehouse, 1976. Continuum, New York.
Vintage Wodehouse, 1977. Barrie & Jenkins, London.
The Swoop and Other Stories, 1979. Continuum, New York.
The Eighteen Carat-Kid and Other Stories, 1980. Continuum, New York
Wodehouse On Wodehouse, 1980. Hutchinson, London,
Wodehouse on Crime, 1981. Ticknor & Fields, New Haven and New York.
Fore! The Best of Wodehouse on Golf, 1983. Ticknor & Fields, New Haven and New York.
P. G. Wodehouse: Four Plays, 1983. Methuen, London.
P. G. Wodehouse: Five Complete Novels, 1985. Avenel, New York.
The Wodehouse Bestiary, 1985. Ticknor & Fields, New York.

First Appearance in Book Form

The Funny Bone, 1928. Scribner's, New York. "Keeping It From Harold."
The Treasure Ship, n.d. Partridge, London. "Pillingshot, Detective."
The Legion Book, 1929. Cassell, London. "Disentangling Old Percy."
The Cecil Alden Book, 1932. Eyre and Spottiswoode, London. "Gone Wrong."
The First Time I —, 1935. Chapman and Hall, London. "Went to New York."
The Laughter Omnibus, 1937. Faber and Faber, London. "The Sluggard."

ALPHABETICAL INDEX OF TITLES*

*Titles in capital letters are books, those in small type are short stories or articles.

275

278

INDEX TO CHARACTERS

281

288

296

305